CHINA
SURVIVAL GUIDE

How to Avoid Travel Troubles and Mortifying Mishaps

Larry and Qin Herzberg

Stone Bridge Press • Berkeley, California

Published by
Stone Bridge Press
P.O. Box 8208
Berkeley, CA 94707
tel 510-524-8732 • sbp@stonebridge.com • www.stonebridge.com

Book design by Linda Ronan.
Front cover illustration by Lloyd Dangle.

Printed in the United States of America.

2012 2011 2010   10 9 8 7 6 5 4

LIBRARY OF CONGRESS CATALOGING-IN-PUBLICATION DATA
Herzberg, Larry.
    China survival guide : how to avoid travel troubles and mortifying mishaps /
Larry and Qin Herzberg. — 1st ed.
        p. cm.
    ISBN 978-1-933330-51-8 (pbk.)
    1. China—Guidebooks. I. Herzberg. Qin. II. Title.
DS705.H47 2007
915.104'6—dc22
              2007014401

Contents

Welcome to China!

Everyone we know is going to China these days. Or so it seems.

There are the business people who now travel frequently to China for their jobs, dealing with everything from office furniture and shoes to Amway products. There are the staff members at our college, who are heading to China to adopt a Chinese baby. The Women's Chorale from our school just returned from performing at Christian churches in Beijing and Xian. Four of our fellow professors, with several of our students to assist them, are about to head to China this summer to tutor English teachers from the Chinese countryside. Each summer we continue to arrange work opportunities for our students in China, that range from teaching English to working in a Chinese company. And then there are the countless friends of ours and parents and grandparents, uncles and aunts of our students, who all either just came back from a two-week trip to China or are just about to go. When we began to teach Chinese at our college in the early 1980s, almost no one was headed for China. Now going to China has become almost as common as a trip to England or

France. China has captured everyone's fancy like never before. As kids, we were told that if we dug a hole in our backyards, sooner or later we'd end up in China. This always made us pause and wonder. Thanks to the miracle of airplane flight, you can now make it to China from anywhere in the United States within 24 hours. And you can arrive without sand in your britches.

Thinking of traveling to China? You're not alone. China now ranks as the third most visited country in the world (up from the 200th or so most visited country in 1970, when China was still "closed" to most foreign visitors). Well over 100 million people from all over the world traveled to China in 2006. Only two million of them were Americans, but that's two million more than went to the "Middle Kingdom" only one generation earlier. After decades of internal and external conflict, China was a geographical and political hot spot. It wasn't until 1971 that President Richard Nixon visited the country, met Mao Zedong, and captured the interest of the West. Economic reforms under Deng Xiaoping just a few years later finally helped open China to American tourists—and McDonald's.

Every culture has its own undisputed contributions to world history of which they can proudly boast. One of China's greatest contributions is its cuisine. If you've never had Chinese food in China, you've simply never really had Chinese food. What's that you say? You can drive over to Chinatown in Manhattan and eat Chinese food 'til the water buffalo come home? It's easy. Why settle for a pale imitation of Peking duck here at home when you can sample the real thing in China. Why eat ordinary pot-stickers,

as they are commonly called in American Chinese restaurants (where they are stuffed only with pork and cabbage), when you can taste hundreds of varieties of *guotie* and *jiaozi*, (savory pan fried and steamed dumplings), amid the colorful streets and alleys of Beijing or Shanghai? Of course, there are other reasons to visit China. There's history, for example. China is a very old place. Dynasties have come and gone. Uncounted millions of people have walked on its soil. While the United States, for instance, tracing its origins back to the earliest settlements in North America, can claim maybe four hundred or so years of history, China has over four thousand. For the history buff, China is the place to see. We Americans do have some important historical sites, but most tend to be small and intimate. China is all about big spaces, and the relationship of man-made objects to their natural surroundings. Nowhere is this more evident than at the Great Wall. Taking in the view at Badaling Pass, one of the more popular spots for tourists, you can see the wall running in the distance, until it goes behind the next hill. Then, you notice

that the wall continues on to the next hill, and the next, and the next, as far as you can see.

Egypt is also an ancient civilization whose historical longevity is on par with China. Take their most famous monuments, the pyramids. These tombs of the Pharaohs are truly among the wonders of the ancient world. But if you get tired of seeing so many tombs all pretty much made in the same shape, visit China for a look at an entirely different kind of tomb. The first emperor of China had a giant mausoleum built for himself beneath the ground with only a gigantic mound to mark the spot. He had around 7,000 life-size clay soldiers made to guard his tomb, each modeled after one of the soldiers in his army. These terra cotta warriors have stood guard in rows buried in the clay of northwest China for 2200 years. When they were unearthed in the mid 1970s, the discovery was called the archaeological find of the century.

You can visit Europe to see many palaces of kings and queens. England has Buckingham Palace, France the magnificent Palace at Versailles, and Germany boasts the Palace of Frederick the Great. None of these countries, however, has a palace that can compare in scope and grandeur to the

Forbidden City in Beijing, home of emperors for more than five hundred years. According to lore it was supposed to have 9,999 rooms (it was said only heaven could have 10,000 rooms), with nine throne rooms. When compared to the terra cotta warriors, for example, The Forbidden City, for all its size and scope, is still relatively "new" as far as Chinese landmarks go. Even though no one lives there today, you can sense the spirits of many generations of Chinese emperors long gone.

China is also worth visiting for the scenery. Like the U.S., which it resembles in size, China has some of the most beautiful and remarkable scenic spots in the world. The kinds of places where your jaw just drops and you try to find words while fumbling for your camera. Enjoy mountains? In China, mountains are sacred places. Huangshan and Taishan are two of the most popular. China borders the Himalayas, of course, but for something more down to earth, take a river cruise to see in real life what you've only seen in photographs: the stunning karst topography of Guilin and the Li River in southern China. There are the unusual mountain formations of Zhangjiajie in Hunan Province, and the aptly-named Stone Forest in Kunming. Few national parks in the U.S. can equal the magnificence of China's Jiuzhaigou National Park, with crystal-clear pure mountain lakes and mountains reminiscent of Glacier National Park. Believe it or not, China also has its own version of the Grand Canyon:

the Nujiang Canyon in Yunnan Province, an area that has often been called Shangri-La. It has also become one of the country's most popular tourist attractions.

Not everyone who visits China is there solely as a tourist. What's the fastest growing economy in the world today? It's China. No matter what your profession, you should be interested in what happens in China. Executives from Tokyo to New York, to London to New Delhi are converging on China; they want to be in on the next "economic miracle."

There are other reasons people visit China. One of the most heartwarming of all is to adopt a Chinese baby, almost all of them are girls. Thousands of people from all over the world have come to China each year to bring a little Chinese child back to their country to be part of their family. Thriving communities of adoptive families and support groups have sprung up all over the world. Even with new, stricter rules for prospective adoptive parents now being put in place, China is still the country with the largest number of overseas adoptions. Every year that we've traveled back to China, we've stayed at a hotel in Beijing where there were many couples from Argentina or the Netherlands or the United States who had just adopted a Chinese toddler and were getting ready to go back home. It was hard to get through the line for the breakfast buffet due to all the strollers spread out all over the dining room. Americans alone adopt between six and seven thousand Chinese youngsters every year. It's wonderful to see these loving, multiracial families that are common all around our West Michigan community.

The majority of visitors to China still travel with a tour group. Everything is arranged. No tickets to buy, no hotel reservations to make, no worrying about what plane or train or bus to take to your next destination, and no lines to stand in. Your tour guide will handle all that for you, and a driver in an air-conditioned bus will take you to all the interesting sites. That's fine for most people, but with more and more solo travelers, couples, or those traveling with family and friends, there is a strong desire to go off the beaten path, away from the air-conditioned buses, and away from the "arranged" tour. If you are one of those people who wants to see China on your own terms, you also have to be able to manage pretty much everything yourself.

You may be taking planes, trains, buses, and taxis. You will need to check yourself into your hotel, order a meal from a restaurant, or buy something in a store. In each case, you will encounter people. All of them (or nearly all) will be Chinese. Depending on where in the country you go, people will speak different dialects. The prevalent dialect is simply called "Guoyü," in places like Taiwan, or "Putonghua," in China (literally: "national language" and "common speech," respectively). This dialect is also commonly called "Mandarin" in English, and is the official language of China.

We've written this book to help inform others, as well as to help us partially re-live the thrill of travel: meeting peo-

ple from a different culture and getting to know them using whatever combination of language and gestures you have at your disposal. The only problem in China is that there are so many people to get to know. Sometimes it seems that at least a million of them are trying to shop in the same market you're shopping in or trying to buy tickets for the same train that you want to take. You came to China wanting to "rub elbows" with the locals, but find that your elbows are a bit sore at the end of each day from all the people you've bumped into walking down the street. Maybe because every Chinese grows up with 1.3 billion other Chinese all around them, they have to learn to push and shove to get on that bus, or to crowd the train ticket window.

In short, not everything is rose-colored when it comes to traveling by yourself in China. There are unique challenges you must face, but should this discourage you from going? Absolutely not! You just need to be psychologically prepared for the little roadblocks of life that China will throw at you. Fortunately, there is nothing terribly serious for the typical tourist to worry about in China. Keep your wits about you, never lose your temper, and above all, keep a sense of humor.

In this book you'll find practical advice for how to make your way through China with good grace. The problems we talk about are for the most part neglected by most travel guidebooks. We tell you what hassles and headaches you might encounter and how to best deal with them. We also try to provide cross-cultural insight as to why those hassles and headaches exist in China in the first place. We hope to help identify potential problems before they affect you; and if you should find yourself in a potentially awkward situation, we hope that we can get you out of it with hopefully very little drama. We like to think our book will prepare you for unexpected cultural encounters by giving you an insider's look at China. Even if you never plan to visit the Middle Kingdom, perhaps you'll enjoy getting a new perspective on a country so different from your own. For those of you who venture to go, just keep in mind the dozens of invaluable tips we provide and you'll come back with nothing but happy memories and lots of great pictures. Let's visit China together in the pages that follow.

Larry and Qin Herzberg
Chinese Language Faculty, Calvin College
Grand Rapids, Michigan, USA

A Note on Pronunciation

In using our Western alphabet to spell Chinese words, we have used two different methods. For each word or phrase we first give the standard transliteration that is now universally accepted. The officially recognized system of romanization is known as hanyu pinyin, or, simply, pinyin. If you've studied Chinese, chances are you'll be able to use pinyin. For those of you new to the Chinese language, we've also included our own unique transliteration of the words in parentheses. This should help you pronounce the words correctly.

Two common Chinese words that are usually pronounced incorrectly here in the U.S. by nearly all television and radio broadcasts, are the words "Beijing" and "yuan." The "j" in the name of China's capital city is not pronounced with the soft "j" sound like *Je suis* in French. The Chinese language lacks that sound entirely. The "j" in "Beijing" is pronounced like the "j" in "Jingle."

The yuan is China's currency, just as the dollar is ours. It is not pronounced "you-anne" or "you-awn." It is pronounced "you-when," or "U.N." said quickly as if it were one syllable.

A User's Guide
to the Chinese Restroom

You've arrived at the airport in China. You feel refreshed and exhilarated after a short ride on the plane directly from your hometown. After all, you slept most of the way on a reclining leather seat the size of a twin bed, and sampled roast pheasant and fine French wine.

This statement might be true if your hometown happens to be Tokyo and you can afford a first class seat. If so, this book might not be for you. More likely, you took a long-haul flight in an economy-class seat from San Francisco, Seattle, or Los Angeles. If you are like us, from the Midwest, then you had an additional flight: from your hometown airport to Chicago, Detroit, Denver, or some other major U.S. hub, then waited for a connection to your international flight. Depending on your carrier, you could be in for anywhere from 10 to 15 hours of total flight time to get to China.

Flights originating overseas can land in Beijing, Shanghai, Guangzhou, Shenzhen, and Chengdu. Beijing Capital Airport or Shanghai Pudong Airport are the major points of entry for most international flights. You disembark from the plane and are ushered into the immigration area. As you shuffle down the corridor, you might encounter a uni-formed officer aiming a gun-like instrument at your fore-head. Don't panic. What this officer is doing is taking ev-eryone's temperature with a state-of-the-art infared digital thermometer. Chances are if anyone is running a high fever, they may be taken aside for medical evaluation before being allowed to enter the country. Seldom do we emerge from a long-haul flight in the best of shape, but the vast majority of travelers have nothing to fear from this seemingly invasive procedure.

By all appearances, most of China's cosmopolitan air-ports are now state of the art structures; they resemble noth-ing like the crumbling, utilitarian buildings of old, which were nothing more than immense waiting rooms practically right on the tarmac itself, where planes roll to a stop within a few feet of the building. Everything about China's new airports gives you the impression that the country has taken great strides at modernizing its infrastructure. Giddy, you suddenly feel a sense of familiarity as if you had just arrived at Denver or San Francisco International. A quick trip to the restroom will put you squarely back in reality. You're in China. Things are different here.

Let's face it, even in an airport, restrooms are important. When you travel anyplace in the world, finding a restroom when Mother Nature calls pretty much tops the list of pri-orities. It's hard to enjoy any part of your trip if you need to

use one but there are none in sight. When it comes to China, talking about restrooms is very important, especially when seconds count. Memorize these characters: 男 (Nán) is male, 女 (Nǚ) is female. Often they may be more prominently displayed than the words "Men" or "Women" or even the familiar gender-specific silhouettes we are accustomed to seeing.

If you're female, and at least half the human race is of that persuasion, then you have a special treat in store at a Chinese airport restroom. You may walk into one of the lovely modern stalls provided for you. Lulled into a sense of security and familiarity by such a modern-looking restroom so far from home, you don't even think to check to see if there is any toilet paper in the stall. That's because in America there are always several giant-sized rolls in industrial-looking acrylic dispensers. That's the problem: your eyes are fooled into thinking that there *must* be an adequate supply of toilet paper. Suddenly, you are in the middle of your business on a Chinese toilet when you realize with horror that there *is* no toilet paper. There may be one of those industrial-looking acrylic dispensers, but it is empty.

The reason is, of course, so obvious that only a West-

erner would fail to understand the logic. If the Chinese provided free toilet paper, what are the chances that someone, sitting out of sight in the stall, would pull out, say, 100 feet of toilet paper from a giant-sized roll and simply carry it home for later use? Obviously, they see the likelihood as very high. The truth is that paper products don't come cheap in China, even if you are a typical worker. The things that we all take for granted are thought of differently.

Now, don't get us wrong: the Beijing and Shanghai airports *do* indeed provide toilet paper, but it's in the logical place—OUTSIDE the toilet stalls, right inside the entrance to the restroom! Any Chinese person knows that, upon entering, you simply need to grab a few pieces of what looks and feels like thin, coarse crepe paper and take it with you into the stall. Better still, you are wise enough to bring your own supply of toilet paper in your purse.

Qin has had the experience of being in a restroom at the Capital City Airport in Beijing when she heard a pathetic cry for help from one of the stalls. The woman was frantically yelling "There is no toilet paper! Please help me!" Qin could see her desperate expression because the woman had actually opened the door to her stall to beg for help. There were at least 15 people in the restroom, plus the female attendant, but no one offered any assistance. Not one to leave a fellow human being in such a pitiful state, Qin hurried to the entrance where the big toilet paper holder for the entire washroom was located. She grabbed a handful of toilet tissue and handed it to the woman.

As far as the men's restrooms are concerned, the same rules apply, that is, should one need to sit. The main difference, however, relates to the ubiquitous male attendant lurking around in the washroom. After you have visited the urinal or stall and make your way to the row of sinks to wash your hands, you will notice this "official-looking" attendant approaching you and offering you, from his pocket, what looks like a towel for you to dry your hands. There are several reasons why we suggest you do not take advantage of what seems a considerate and selfless act:

- The so-called "towel" is really thin tissue of dubious origin.
- The paper is so thin it literally falls apart in your hands.
- If you look around the restroom, you'll notice that even though there are no paper towels, there is an electric hand dryer attached to the wall that you can use for free.
- Most importantly, if you do accept the gesture of

service the attendant offers you, he will then expect
that you will tip him accordingly.

If you plan on doing a lot of sightseeing, know that most
public restrooms in China do not provide toilet paper at all.
Chinese people know to always carry their own supply. It's
a good idea to keep a small supply with you at all times.
You can take a roll along from your hotel room if you have
room to carry it. Be aware, though, that Chinese hotels are
very stingy in usually giving you only one or two very small
rolls. If you want to buy your own supply on the street, it is
relatively easy to find small "convenience-store" type shops
that sell all manner of bathroom supplies and toiletries.

Most public restrooms in China do not provide you with
soap either. They also rarely offer hot water from the tap.
You will need to bring your own supply of "wet wipes" or
a bottle of hand sanitizer to use throughout the day. Many
public restrooms in China do not provide either paper towels or a hand dryer, although a lot more of them provide a
dryer than provide toilet paper or soap! It's not a bad idea
to carry a handkerchief with you to dry your hands. Many
public toilets in China are still of the infamous "squat" variety, though in recent years there has been a marked increase
in "sit-down" Western-style toilets these days. The aptly-
named "squatty-potties," as we affectionately call them,
require that you squat on your haunches over a hole in the
floor. Keep in mind that many of these toilets are of the flush

variety—it's not like a port-a-potty at the state fair. If you're lucky, there will be porcelain inlay on either side of the hole. This is where your feet should go.

The "squatty potties" have never found favor in the West, which is strange since they do have a practical advantage over the toilets we're used to. Since your bottom doesn't actually touch a place touched by the bottoms of countless other people, the hygienic issue for the most part is a non-starter. The vast majority of Chinese people prefer this kind of toilet for this very reason, even when given the choice between squatting and sitting on a toilet seat. Since toilet seat covers are considered a useless luxury and your supply of toilet paper is already limited, you also don't have to worry about covering the seat before you sit down if you were using a western toilet. Given the fact that there is usually no air conditioning in public restrooms in China, the inside of a restroom often resembles a sauna. If you do cover a western-style toilet seat with toilet paper, upon arising when the deed is done you will find that all the aforementioned paper is now stuck to your rear.

The main problem with the "squatty potties," and it *is* a

big problem, is that they simply have not found a place in the Western *aesthetic de toilette*. In China, where things are usually slow to change, this can mean a long, fruitless search for a familiar-looking toilet. In many public restrooms in China there is no choice: all the stalls for men and women are of the squat variety. The nicer the restaurant or the more famous the historical site, temple, or museum you visit, the more likely it is that the restroom will have a Western-style toilet somewhere behind one of the many stall doors. Increasingly there are pictures on the stall doors indicating the type of toilet you'll find inside. Our advice is to not immediately get discouraged upon opening the stall door to find a "squatty potty." Do not give up until you've tried every stall in your quest for a pleasant experience.

With the building of the new wing of the Beijing Capital Airport, in preparation for the 2008 Summer Olympics, there are now public restrooms on a par with the best in the West. But these are still the exception in China.

Never Take a Black Cab and Other Taxi Tips

Having used the restroom, you retrieve your luggage from the very modern and up-to-date baggage carousel in the airport. You've been cleared through immigration and customs and you're now ready to take a taxi into town. This will be the first of many taxi rides you will probably take in China. As we'll talk about later, many Chinese are just itching to take a foreigner, literally and figuratively, for "a ride." Taxis are everywhere. There are around sixty thousand in Beijing alone and thirty or forty thousand in Shanghai. Taxis are also much cheaper than in America.

Not only will you probably take a taxi from the airport to your hotel, you will probably be taking taxis to get around in the city. There are plenty of public buses, but most are filled with locals packed in like sardines. It is a unique experience for most foreigners to be in a bus pressed in so tightly by other human bodies that you feel yourself lifted off your feet. Most cities don't have subway systems. The few subway systems that do exist in Beijing and Shanghai barely cover a fraction of the city. So cabs are generally the best way to get around.

You can hail a taxi on any well-traveled street in any Chinese city. In the busier places of cities like Shanghai we've stood on a street corner and counted as many as 30 taxis pass us in the space of exactly 60 seconds. In most places in China, taxis all charge the same bargain price of 10 yuan for the first three kilometers and then 1.6 yuan for every kilometer after that.

However, in Beijing prices were a bit more complicated up until 2008. Here there were three different classes of taxis, with rates respectively of 1.20 yuan, 1.60 yuan, and 2.00 yuan. If you took one of the taxis at 1.20 yuan, it would be cheaper, of course. But these cabs were usually smaller, older, and shabbier looking than the more expensive ones. More importantly, on one of those all-too-common 90-plus degree days in the summer, these cheap cabs usually did not have air conditioning.

During 2008, with the approach of the Olympics, all but the 2-yuan cabs in Beijing were phased out. The 2-yuan cabs all have air conditioning. Just make sure the driver turns it on. He might be trying to save gas by leaving it off. This is commendable in that it helps conserve a precious natural resource and cuts down on pollution. Politely utter the magic words "kōng-tiáo" (pronounced "kung tee-ow"), or, "qǐng kāi lěng qì" (pronounced "ching kai lung chee," or "please turn on the air conditioning"), and the driver will usually oblige. Be sure to take down the number of your taxi, so you can report him if he "takes you for a ride" or if you leave something valuable in the cab that you need to retrieve.

Just as with most Western airports, the taxi stand is right outside the airport arrival hall doors. On your way to lining up at the official taxi stand you very likely will be approached by a friendly man who will offer you a ride into town. You assume that he's a taxi driver and that if you take his cab you can save precious minutes waiting in line. This would be a bad decision. This man most likely is the driver of a "hei che" (pronounced "hay-chuh") or, literally, "black car." By "black" the Chinese mean "dark," "nefarious," and, therefore, "illegal." As if to live up their name, the cars these drivers use are generally black, to avoid attention, a direct contrast to the colorful, eye-catching look we've come to associate with taxis worldwide. The drivers of the "black cars" have not paid the money for a taxi license and belong to no taxi company. That means their car will have no meter and they will charge you whatever they like for the ride. Some tourists have been told when finally reaching their hotel after a circuitous "scenic route" that they owed thousands of

yuan. Usually one ends up paying several hundred yuan for a ride in a "black car," instead of the 90 or 100 yuan you'd pay for a real taxi. Ignore all offers of a ride and wait in line at the cab stand. Just follow the crowd. Another advantage of standing in line at the cab stand is that there are government workers standing there to direct you to a cab. They will write down the number of the cab and the driver who will be taking you into the city, and hand that information to you. In case you have any complaint or leave anything in the taxi, you'll have some recourse.

Now might be a good time to discuss tipping in China. The good news is that it isn't the custom to tip for most of the services you'll receive. That includes taxi rides. Taxi drivers in the U.S. need the promise of a tip to give them the incentive to drive you quickly and safely to your destination. The Chinese cab driver needs no other reward beyond the fee on the meter . . . and, of course, the great delight in watching through the rear-view mirror the panic-stricken look on the face of the foreign tourist as the cab weaves in and out of lanes at breakneck speed, defying death at every turn. In recent years a large number of Chinese people, including the elderly, have come to depend on taxis as a reasonably priced and easy way to get around. If foreigners tip cabbies so that they come to expect it, cabs will become pricier for locals. When we have offered to let the cabby "keep the change" when paying, he has always politely but firmly refused, saying they're not allowed to accept tips.

Tipping is also not customary in restaurants. Unlike the U.S., where we need to tip "to insure promptness and good service," most countries in the world automatically add the tip to the bill. In fancier restaurants in China a gratuity of 15% is routinely added.

There are times when a tip is expected in China. The porters in the hotels expect a tip of ten yuan (a little over a dollar) for helping you up to your room with your bags. Unlike in the U.S., however, if you fail to tip them they will simply leave the room. They won't stand there with their palm up explaining every feature of your room until you pay them to stop, as is the custom in America. It is also expected that if you hire a private driver and a guide to take you around, you will give the driver around fifty yuan extra and the guide a hundred yuan as a tip. That's because these people are used to serving only foreign tourists. They know all too well our American custom and think it's a dandy idea.

3

How to Stand in Line and Not Have a Cow

As the Chinese themselves will constantly tell you: "China has too many people!" It's a daily mantra repeated by all Chinese, from taxi drivers to university professors. For some reason, and we're not sure exactly why, the vast majority of China's population have never learned the concept of lining up in an orderly fashion. Unless you see it for yourself you simply won't believe it. People in Western countries generally consider the law of "queuing up" absolute, and woe to anyone who thinks otherwise. So do the Japanese, for that matter. Even in Hong Kong, proud former British colony that it is, the locals (who, let's face it, have been known more for their pursuit of wealth than their people-friendly skills) still look down with scorn at their "backward" country cousins across the border who seemingly don't know the meaning of lining up in an orderly way.

Perhaps it's because Chinese people have always had two sets of rules when it comes to how to treat others. They treat their friends and family with the greatest care and concern. They treat strangers with total indifference, and courtesy goes out the window. Or perhaps it's because there are just too many people wanting the same goods and services. The feeling is that if you don't push and shove  to make it to the head of the line, you'll probably have to wait all day for what you want. And it doesn't help that for the first thirty years of Communist rule, there was no concern with etiquette or manners. It was a society that took pride in attacking anyone and anything that was refined. Refined manners, after all, belonged to the former ruling class of aristocrats and scholars.

In any case, never näively think that you can just line up behind the folks ahead of you, secure in the knowledge that the people behind you will courteously *stay* behind you. You will soon discover that not just one person but often a number of them will try to get ahead of you in line. Even if you leave just a foot of space between you and the person in front, you'll often find that somehow or other a person has rushed in from parts unknown and managed to squeeze himself or herself into that foot of space. So get close to the person standing in front of you in line. Real close. Close enough to see if they shampooed this morning.

The caveat here is to use your best judgment when in a

situation like this. Try to blend in and don't make a scene. Don't yell or rant. It sometimes seems as if watching foreigners crack under the relentless pressure of Chinese society is a favorite pastime among the locals. It doesn't matter whether you are waiting for a taxi at the airport, queuing up at an airline counter, buying tickets of any kind, or checking in or out of a hotel. There is a fine line between blending in and doing as the locals do, and becoming so frustrated with it all that becoming an Ugly American seems like the only way to get anything done.

What to Expect
(and Inspect) at Your Hotel

China now has a large number of four and five-star hotels in all the major tourist locations. You will have no trouble finding a very comfortable place to stay in the Middle Kingdom, although these days the prices can be almost as high as for an equivalent hotel in the U.S. In addition to the recognized Western chain hotels, there are numerous domestic hotels, catering mainly to a Chinese clientele. The latter can be a bargain if you know what to look for. Remember, of course, that what is called a five-star hotel in China would only be rated as probably a three or four-star hotel in America; a four-star hotel in China would only garner two or three stars here, etc. If a hotel has a one-star rating, you are probably better off sleeping on the street. Nevertheless, finding a nice place to lay your tired body down in the land of the Great Wall should not be a problem.

Checking the Name of Your Hotel

If your local travel agency arranges your trip through a travel agency in China, which is the usual practice, make

sure you don't just get the English name of your hotel. Get the Chinese name of the hotel as well, so you can show it to the driver, along with the correct address. The problem here is that the English and Chinese names of hotels are not literal translations of each other, and English names of a large number of hotels often bear little or no resemblance to the meaning of the Chinese name.

Checking Your Room

Once you arrive safely at your hotel and check-in, you figure you can finally relax now. You can't wait to unpack, shower, change clothes, and begin exploring. Wrong, wrong, wrong! First check carefully to see if everything in your room is in working order!

The biggest problem you encounter with Chinese hotel rooms, even if you're staying in a five-star hotel, is that inevitably something will be wrong with the room. It won't be something terribly serious, like having a hole in the wall, but something will be amiss, even if you don't notice it at first glance. And in every hotel it will be something different.

The reason something is probably not quite right with your room is that most buildings in China are put up very hastily and as cheaply as possible; they have to be in order to keep up with the incredible construction boom. This is a classic paradox: on the one hand, the building (or hotel room) will seem beautiful, but this is often a façade concealing shoddy construction and poor attention to detail. There is little concern for a little something we in America like to call QC, or "quality control." This is slowly changing, but because of shoddy design and workmanship, a hotel only five years old can (and often does) resemble something two decades old or more. Anything that can possibly break most likely will; either a switch will not operate or a latch won't work right. You need to check that everything is working, especially the basic things like the faucets and the toilet. Make sure that the sink and the shower don't leak and that the shower drain actually allows water to escape from the tub. Check that the air conditioner really puts out cold air. Look to see if there are washcloths in the bathroom. Most Chinese staying in hotels aren't accustomed to using those handy little towels we Americans depend on to soap ourselves with, so Chinese hotels often fail to put them out automatically for guests unless you ask for them. If there are no washcloths or anything else is missing, you can always call the number listed by the phone for "Housekeeping." Ask for "xiǎo fāngjīn" (pronounced "see-ow fahng-jin"), which is Chinese for "little square towel."

There is one good thing about Chinese hotels that have at least a four-star rating. The staff is quick to answer your call for help, since they expect there will be problems. It's likely they wait by the phone, crouched down in the position runners assume at the beginning of a race. They know that any minute the phone will ring with another complaint. And they're almost always really friendly and anxious to remedy the situation. In our experience the staff usually arrived within two minutes of our call. This is pretty impressive in light of the fact that we've stayed in around fifty hotels in China and probably made around a hundred calls for help!

While you're checking that everything in your hotel room is in working order, look for soap. Many Chinese hotels provide one tiny biscuit of soap for you to use in the sink. But for the bath they often provide a very small plastic bottle of liquid soap. Personally we consider these miniscule bottles of liquid soap a real pain, since all you can squeeze out onto your washcloth is a little dribble and its hard to get a good lather going. If like us you would prefer to use a bar of soap in the shower, call "Housekeeping" and say the magic word "xiāngzào" (seeahng-dzow).

Below is a "small" list of some of the things that might be wrong with your room. We'll include the snafus mentioned above just so you'll have a complete list. We know from personal experience these things need to be checked, because the items below cover the problems we encountered in hotels just on our last trip around China. We include these because they are all common problems, and they're still fresh in our mind. By the way, we only stayed in "four-star" hotels arranged for us by China's premiere travel agency.

- leak under the sink
- leak in the bathtub
- bathtub drain not working: Don't wait until you're taking your first shower to find this out. You could be up to your armpits in water before you get all the shampoo out of your eyes!
- faucet in the sink keeps dripping, or even pouring out water
- air conditioning not working (usually it's not plugged in)
- air conditioning vent leaking water from condensation
- stink in the hallway from recent painting or other remodeling work
- safe not working—either won't lock or won't open
- water boiler not working
- mini refrigerator not plugged in
- TV cable not connected, so no TV reception

- dead (or missing) batteries in TV remote control; not functional
- no light to read by: either some lights are burned out or the bulbs they put in are only ten or twenty watts
- not enough or no towels, washcloths, or soap

In fact as soon as you enter your hotel room you might be convinced that nothing works at all. You try to turn on the lights and—nothing happens. That's because you have to take your room key card and insert it in a slot near the door for anything electrical to work. In a nation like China where electrical power is at a premium, the hotel needs to make sure that you don't leave all the lights on in the room when you leave for the day. Europeans have learned the wisdom of this and use the same type of system in many of their hotels. We Americans, however, like the idea of returning to a hotel room that's all lit up, so everything will seem very homey and inviting when we get back from visiting the Great Wall. The Chinese just don't have electric power to burn, so to speak. So get used to inserting that key card before flicking any switches.

The ubiquitous "bedside console" is legend in Chinese hotel room lore. A combination nightstand/reading table and "mission control" center for your room, there are numerous switches that can control (so it is said) the TV, radio, reading and room lights, alarm clock, etc. We've never found the consoles to work well, but if you like pushing buttons, they are a lot of fun.

Drinking Water

When you travel it's essential to stay hydrated. Human beings can go for a long time without food, but we can't live for long without water. When you're traveling your body has to work harder to get used to new surroundings; you do a lot more walking and expend a lot more energy than you would ordinarily. In addition, most of us tend to do our traveling in China during the hot summer months, when almost all the large Chinese cities often see temperatures between 90 and 100 degrees, with very high humidity. When traveling in China or anywhere else in the world, carrying a supply of water around with you on each day's outing is absolutely essential.

The problem here is that in the great majority of countries in the world it is not safe to drink the tap water without boiling it first. China is one of those countries. NEVER DRINK THE TAP WATER IN ANY HOTEL IN CHINA, or anywhere else in the country, for that matter. A large number of hotels provide you with two bottles of "mineral water" which is safe to drink. And it's free. However, many of us can finish the contents of these bottles in two or three gulps. Many hotels instead provide you with a small water cooler/heater that contains water they've boiled for you. After you use up that supply, which can perhaps fill four glasses,

you can always refill it yourself with tap water and press the switch to boil the water in this little contraption. That's time consuming, however, and still doesn't give you a large "reservoir" of drinking water for your daily excursions outside of your hotel.

The good news is that the Chinese people all have the same problem you have with obtaining clean, safe drinking water. There are, therefore, countless small shops on almost every street in China where you can purchase large bottles of drinking water for a very reasonable price. There are many decent brands, but our personal favorite is called "Wa Ha Ha." The title is from a popular song and means "baby laughing." What better name for bottled water than "Laughing Baby." It calls up happy memories of those baths our mothers gave us as little children, when they poured water all over us and got shampoo in our eyes. Of course, you can pay for the extra bottles of mineral water in your hotel room or in the hotel gift shop. But their prices are often three times what you'd pay "on the street." And in China a small shop with water, toilet paper, and other daily necessities is rarely more than a block away.

If you're buying water outside the hotel, however, it is

crucial that you keep in mind the following rule: always buy water from a store. Never purchase water from some person just standing around on the street if they only have a small number of bottles spread out in front of them on a tarp, or even behind a small stand. Even if the water looks perfectly clear, it's very likely these people have simply filled some empty bottles with tap water and skillfully resealed them. We're not kidding. Friends of ours have gotten very sick drinking water they bought in this way while traveling.

The Breakfast Buffet

When you stay at any decent hotel in China, a buffet breakfast in the dining room is always included in the price of your room. That's because, although China has gotten civilized enough to have hundreds of McDonald's, Kentucky Fried Chickens, and even Starbucks, they are not yet so enlightened as to boast a Bob Evans or an International House of Pancakes. This leaves many of us without a decent place to go for eggs and ham, let alone pancakes. Answer: the "free" breakfast buffet.

At the time you check into your hotel you'll be given coupons for each morning's meal. They tell you that you can head to the dining room for breakfast any time between the hours of 6:30 and 10:00 A.M. So you get up the next morning and head down to breakfast at the reasonable time of 8:30. The young hostess at the entrance eyes you suspiciously as you approach. Obviously you're some freeloader who's wandered in having smelled something cooking. You smugly hand over your carefully guarded tickets to show you belong there after all but the hostess gives you a dirty look. Seems in your morning grogginess you've handed her two losing Lotto tickets by mistake. When you finally fish out the coveted meal coupons, she waves you in curtly. But it seems you're on your own when it comes to finding a table.

You figure you'll get your food first and then find a place to sit. So you head for the buffet tables. Then you notice the crowd of guests that look like a delegation from the United Nations.

There are tourists from every part of the world. You think you see other Americans but it turns out they speak Russian, or German. There are also more and more domestic tourists coming from other parts of China. It seems like they're all descending on the food like a swarm of locusts. Who can blame them after all that airline food? Like acrobats the diners are all balancing two or three plates in their hands, and if they could balance a plate on their head, they probably would. They scurry from place to place desperately seizing anything in sight. So you do the only rational thing. You join them.

The breakfast items are usually segregated into "Asian" and "Western" sections. The former will almost always feature several variations of the ever-popular rice gruel, cold cuts of seemingly unfamiliar meat, noodles, steamed dim sum, braised fish with black beans, and a host of other food items, some of which you may have never seen before.

The Western section is usually larger. There are typically cold cuts of seemingly unfamiliar meat, slices of cheese, a chafing dish of scrambled eggs, pancakes, potatoes or hash browns (or some variation thereof), sausage or bacon, and several kinds of toast and pas-

tries. There is usually a good selection of fruit (some fresh, some canned) as well as a cereal bar for health conscious Europeans and Americans where one can even find their beloved muesli and Rice Krispies respectively.

You go over to a chafing dish labeled "Germany potatoes." English translation: "German-style potatoes." You lift the lid to take some and it seems you've grown a third hand. Maybe it's something in the water in China! But sure enough there it is—a hand appearing in front of you helping itself to a generous portion of the potatoes before your tongs ever touch the tubers! It's every diner for himself, it seems.

In any four- or five-star hotel in China there will invariably be an omelette chef, hidden in some corner of the dining room. Be sure to look around for him, because the Chinese really know how to prepare eggs, along with just about everything else. The young chef has a skillet in front of him and he holds a metal spatula in his hand. "Omelettes!" you shout with glee over the din of the dining room and make a mad dash for eggs. Unfortunately there are already five tourists ahead of you, all holding an empty plate in front of them. You recall the touching scene in the musical "Oliver" where the young boy holds out his porridge dish and with a pitiful voice mutters "Please, sir . . . I'd like some more." Ten minutes later, juggling several plates and a tiny bowl of cereal, you and your companion look for a place to sit. It's then that you notice that there are no empty tables!

Almost all the tour groups are scheduled to meet at 9:00 down in the Lobby for their daily excursion and so everyone pours into the dining room between eight and nine each morning. Our advice: Get up at 5:30 or 6:00, when the Chinese do, and be the first foreigners down to breakfast. That way you'll have the first chance to grab the potatoes. Or wait until the veritable locust swarm is gone after 9:00 for a sure bet at a table. Of course all the melon slices and bananas might be gone too, but you'll be able to sit where you like.

Exchanging Money

Money may be the "root of all evil" but somehow it's hard to buy anything in China without it. The Chinese call their currency the yuan. Your hotel in China gives you the chance to exchange money right in the lobby. The exchange rate you'll get will be no worse than what the banks offer. That's because often the hotels are providing a service on behalf of the banks, or the local bank will actually set up shop inside the hotel for this purpose. For the past few decades the exchange rate has hardly fluctuated at all. The Chinese government artificially kept the rate at around 8.2 yuan per U.S. dollar. The U.S. government tried unsuccessfully for years to get the Chinese government to raise the value of the yuan to a market value of around six yuan to the dollar. Only in the summer of 2005 did the Chinese finally allow the yuan to increase in value slightly. When changing money there's a point when shopping around for the best rate becomes a ridiculous pursuit; there's no point worrying over a few tenths of a percentage point. The official exchange rate at the time this book was written is approximately 6.8 yuan per dollar, but with the usual commission fee you'll end up with no more than around 6.5 yuan. You'll get pretty much this same rate no matter where you exchange your money.

The big question we're all faced with when we travel is: cash or traveler's checks? Of course traveler's checks are safer to carry around, but cash is simpler. Whether you exchange traveler's checks or cash, you will have to show your passport. You do get a slightly better exchange rate with traveler's checks, but they deduct a bigger commission with the checks so you end up with pretty much the same amount of money either way.

The next big question is where should you exchange

your money? Unless you're traveling with a tour group where transportation has already been arranged for you, you'll need Chinese currency to take a taxi. Fortunately the major Chinese airports have exchange counters in the arrivals area, and they'll be able to handle a currency exchange very quickly and efficiently. After that, the most convenient (and quickest) way to exchange money is at the front desk of your hotel. However, whether you exchange cash or traveler's checks, just realize that many hotels will not let you exchange more than $200 per transaction. You may, however, exchange money many times a day at the same hotel, just not all at once.

Some hotels will also not accept traveler's checks but only cash. Other hotels will let you exchange cash at any time, but have limited hours for exchanging traveler's checks, such as from 2:00 P.M. to 5:00 P.M.! You may always exchange either traveler's checks or cash at a bank, but only at the Bank of China, since no other Chinese banks allow foreign currency exchange. It takes much longer to exchange money at a bank than at your hotel, but at least it's orderly. Be sure to take a number as you enter the door and watch for your number to come up above the tellers' windows. Be warned, however. It often takes so much time to transact any business in a bank, and the Chinese people are constantly complaining to the government about it. For the sake of convenience, it is definitely better to exchange your money at your hotel. Unlike Europe or Hong Kong, there are unfortunately no money exchange centers on the street in China.

If you do decide to bring cash to exchange for Chinese dollars, make sure you get the bank in your country to give you nice, crisp, new-looking bills. On our most recent trip we had gotten mostly $50 and $100 bills from our bank in Michigan, thinking that we would only need to carry a small handful of money that way and the exchange would be quicker. Neither the teller at our bank nor we cared that the bills were a bit creased, but when we went to exchange our $50 and $100 bills at the money exchange table of our four-star hotel in Xiamen (Fujian Province), we were told that they could not accept old bills like the ones we had.

This becomes especially important when we tell you that you'll mostly need cash to pay for things in China. Elegant restaurants or big department stores will accept credit cards, but China is still mostly a cash culture. Even many restaurants or stores that certainly look big and fancy enough to accept credit cards expect you to pay in cash. Meals are typically not expensive, and you may well find that paper money can go a long way.

Another thing to keep in mind is that if you use cash for your transactions (usually 100 yuan notes), more often than not the shopkeeper, taxi driver, or whoever you give

your money to will hold the bill carefully up to the light, scrutinizing it to see if it's fake. Don't be embarrassed or take it as a personal insult that all Chinese automatically assume a foreigner would be an unwitting carrier of fake currency. While banks have more discreet ways of checking a bill's authenticity, most people just want to play it safe.

ATMs that will accept foreign bank cards or credit cards are not easy to find in China outside of the largest cities like Beijing, Shanghai, and Guangzhou. If you plan on using a credit card for purchases as well as for trying to get money out of an ATM, you will need to contact your card company to ask them to honor transactions made in China, giving them the dates when you'll be in the country. Another problem with the ATM machine you may encounter is that the display on the screen, as well as all the buttons (with the exception of the numbers) are in Chinese. Not all ATMs are programmed to display non-Chinese characters. While the machine may look familiar from a distance, once you get up to it you may not be able to figure out how it works. Avoid the embarrassing situation of figuring out how to get your card back once you've put it in the machine and can't figure out which button to push.

Our advice is to forget about ATMs outside of Beijing and Shanghai. Use credit cards to pay for hotels, meals in fancier restaurants, and purchases of expensive souvenirs in stores, but take enough cash along to pay for everything else.

The good news is that as long as you keep your money along with your passport and other valuables in a money belt or fanny pack, it is still safer to carry around a lot of cash in China than it is in Europe or America. In China there are still no purse-snatchers on motorbikes, such as we've seen in Italy, or teams of pickpockets who bump into you to take your money while you're distracted, such as we've experienced ourselves in Prague. Estimate the amount of money you'll need for admission fees to major attractions, meals in small restaurants, snacks and drinking water, taxis or buses, and small souvenir presents, and bring enough cash. Tourists in China run the gamut from the frugal, unshaven backpacker to the traveler who goes first class all the way. We've found that US$300 per week is more than enough for the average person, since things like food and taxis are still very inexpensive in China by western standards.

Keeping Your Money Safe

Despite (or, perhaps, because of) its population, China is a very safe society when it comes to personal safety. You're more likely to be mugged in your own backyard in the U.S. than late at night on the streets of Beijing or Shanghai. Though many European countries have more pickpockets than China, you still need to be careful with your valuables, including your money as well as your passport and airplane tickets. Chinese criminals generally don't like to deal with foreigners, and certainly any kind of robbery or assault type crime is extremely rare. Of course, if you are stumbling drunk down the street with you wallet half hanging out of your back pocket, you may just be too good a target for a petty criminal to resist. For the most part, however, keep your wits about you and you'll be fine.

Fortunately most four-star hotels in China have a small safe in the room that you're free to use. It's carefully concealed in the closet or mounted directly inside the wall. If the safe is in working order, though, it's not a bad place to stash your most valuable things except for the cash you think you'll need for that day's adventure.

Laundry

When traveling, sooner or later you're going to be faced with the necessity of washing some of your clothes. There are a number of ways out of this dilemma, of course. It's cheap to buy new clothing in China, which is not surprising since most products in the garment industry are made there and exported to the West. A good idea is to use the laundry service at your hotel. While this is sadly no longer the bargain it once was in the "good old days" of the 1980s, it's still the most cost-effective and convenient way of dealing with the situation.

Here are typical laundry prices at an average four-star hotel in China:

dress shirt: 15 yuan (about US$1.85)
cotton dress: 15 yuan
long dress: 15 yuan
blouse: 15 yuan
"normal" shirt: 14 yuan (about US$1.75)
sport shirt: 13 yuan (about US$1.60)
men's slacks: 10 yuan (about US$1.25)
women's slacks: 16–20 yuan (US$2.50)
underpants: 5 yuan (US$.60)
socks: 5 yuan

The hotel provides a bag for laundry and a form, in both English and Chinese, in which you list the number of each item you want washed. Supposedly you just leave that bag of dirty clothes in your room before you leave in the morning and you'll get it back in the evening on your return from that day's adventures, neatly folded and fresh-smelling.

So far this seems to differ little from the system that American hotels use for guests to get their laundry done. What is different in the Chinese case is that the employees in a Chinese hotel might attempt to inspect every piece of clothing with you present before the wash is done and then

again after the wash is returned. They want to make sure that the number and type of item is exactly what you have put on the form. That is because these employees are personally responsible should a guest claim they put in a Ralph Lauren dress shirt and got back a laundered T-shirt with "Joe's Garage" on the back. So be prepared for the Chinese hotel staff to dump out all your dirty clothes on your bed and check each item against the checklist you filled out, and then again check each laundered item with you when they return everything in the evening. You will agree, however, that this gives you a lovely half hour in which to get to know some very nice young Chinese people, with whom you can discuss in halting English such heady topics as the difference between a dress shirt and a sport shirt.

There is something to be said for this way of handling the laundry as opposed to the 1980s in China. At that time the hotel would provide you with a long explanation in very creative English that warned the guest that should your "count" of the number of items to be laundered differ from the hotel's "count," the hotel's "count" would be assumed by the hotel to be correct and not your "count," and they would charge you accordingly. So if you said you had five shirts, but the hotel counted 50 shirts, they would charge you for laundering 50 shirts.

One hotel we stayed at in southern China in the early 1980s had an explanation similar to that above, namely: "should your count differ from our count, then our count will be assumed to be correct and not your count." The only difference was, on the printed notice, they had inadvertently left out the letter "o" from "count."

Elevators

Elevators work the same all over the world. What's different about elevators in China is the set of rules for entering and exiting the elevators. If you're an American in China, you must learn a whole new set of elevator rules from those you operated under back home. In a city in the U.S., for instance, when an elevator arrives at a floor and the door opens, the people who are waiting for the elevator generally let the people who are getting off the elevator actually get off the elevator before entering the elevator themselves. There is also a sense of fair play among Americans that, while they generally do not stand in line for an elevator, whoever arrived in front of the elevator first deserves to get on the elevator first. In China you can just forget all of the above.

Dealing with elevators can be a frustrating experience, and, along with the seeming futility of standing in line, can (and occasionally does) bring out the worst in tourists un-used to the social landscape. The incessant crowding, the seeming disregard for decorum and "proper" behavior, will soon have you playing the "Ugly American" card. Just relax and don't take it personally. Use your space and protect it. It's OK to push and jostle, but above all keep your cool and don't lose your temper.

Massage in the Hotels

Massage, a form of traditional Chinese medicine, has a long history and is all the rage in China. Everywhere you go there are places advertising almost every kind of massage therapy imaginable. Foot massage is still one of the most popular forms of massage, and you'll see signs everywhere for places that offer that kind of service. Almost all the ho-tels offer a large selection of massage choices, from full body massage of various kinds to different kinds of foot massage, and everything in between. Usually the hotel will have a "spa" or a designated space offering massage services. Most of the time it's a perfectly legitimate service operated by experienced and trained professionals. If, however, you're offered massage in your room, you need to realize that there is a slippery slope between legitimate massage therapy and another kind of massage. For those of us seeking relief from a sore back or sore feet at the end of the tourist day, the "massage" they're really offering may not be what the doc-tor ordered . . . unless the doctor is Dr. Ruth! In many hotels, as soon as a man enters his hotel room at night, within a minute or two his phone will ring. He picks it up and hears the sweet voice of a young woman with  a simple question: "Yào àn mó ma?" (Would you like a massage?). One can only assume that the mystery caller(s) are in cahoots with the front desk staff, and possibly even operate with their blessing. It happened to us even when we were together as a couple in a very respectable hotel in Shanghai. It was only when Larry mentioned the Chinese word for police (jǐngchá) that the caller finally hung up.

Regardless of whatever you may be offered in your room, the authentic "medicinal foot bath and massage" is 100% legitimate and is a true balm to your tired dogs as well as to your spirit. This we highly recommend. Most Chinese hotels employ a small army of young women from the countryside who have been trained for a few weeks in how to take all the pain out of overworked feet and make them whole again. The young woman will first bathe your foot in a small tub of hot water into which she has placed different aromatic Chinese herbs. This is supposedly to relax and soothe your foot, helping it to heal with ancient mountain herbal remedies perfected over centu-

ries by Taoist monks in remote temples on distant mountains. More likely the real purpose is to make your foot odor less severe so that the masseuse can bear to get near it! After a few minutes of soaking in the piping hot medicinal soup, the masseuse will start massaging every part of your aching and overworked feet. After a few minutes, you realize that this is good for both your sole and your soul.

Staying in Touch

At some point during your travels around China, you'll find yourself missing your loved ones back home and wanting to share your adventures with them. You'll be tempted to call them from the telephone so conveniently located next to your bed in your hotel room. This would be a big mistake. As in hotels around the world, Chinese hotels also charge you a few U.S. dollars a minute to reach out and touch someone back in your home country. With the money it would cost you to talk for several hours to a few of your friends and family members, you could almost afford to fly back home to see them!

There are several very good alternatives. One is to have

your loved ones call you, using an international phone card. These are available now at a supermarket near you. The cheapest phone cards for calls to China are easily purchased online from any number of websites, including www. ecallchina.com and www.sinocalling.com. We have found these to be reliable and secure sites. Within a few minutes of purchasing one of these phone cards online with a credit card, you will be sent an e-mail with the access number to call and your pin number. With these phone cards it costs a mere two or three cents a minute to call China from the United States, any day at any time. Just be sure your friends and family are aware of the time difference between North America and China. Since all of China is in one time zone even though the country is as wide and large as the U.S., and since China does not use daylight savings time, China is 12 hours later than Eastern Standard time from the first day of spring until the first day of fall, and is 13 hours later from the first day of fall until the following first day of spring. If, for example, you call Beijing or Shanghai from San Francisco or Los Angeles at 8:00 P.M. on New Year's Eve, it will already be noon of New Year's Day in China!

Another easy and relatively inexpensive way to stay in touch with your loved ones is by e-mail. Almost every hotel in China these days has a Business Center on the first floor with broadband internet access that you can use to send and read e-mail. The more expensive the hotel, the more they charge for 1 hour of use, although they will pro-rate the charges by 15-minute increments. Here you can expect to pay between $4 and $8 U.S. to use one of their computers.

For a cheaper and more interesting alternative to getting internet access, try one of the more than 100,000 internet cafes, or "Wang Ba" ("Internet Bars") located all over China. Here the rates are usually as cheap as $1 or $1.50 U.S. per hour. You'll find these kinds of internet cafes or bars on main streets in every Chinese city and even in small towns that are major tourist places. We were delighted to find an internet bar in the tiny town of Dali, nestled in the mountains of Yunnan Province not far from Tibet. They had eight computers, and, after waiting a few minutes for a Chinese teenager to finish playing video games on one of them, we were able to check our e-mail back in Michigan for around 80 cents an hour.

Thanks to the miracle of the internet and e-mail, you can stay in touch with those you care about from most parts of the globe almost instantly. In China, more than one hundred million Chinese access the internet, and millions of Chinese now own computers. A much larger number of Chinese take advantage of the cafés that make internet use accessible and affordable.

A Walker's Guide to China's Streets

Hotels in China that accommodate foreigners tend to be not only very large, but also self-contained. Many foreigners who come to China on business rarely leave their hotel except for their scheduled business meetings. More than just providing you with a place to rest your weary head at night, large hotels in China offer a choice of restaurants, many small shops for souvenirs and daily necessities, a recreation center, a business center with computers and FAX machines, and laundry service—everything to meet your daily needs. Of course if you really want to see what China is all about, you're going to eventually need to leave the hotel and venture out into the streets.

The Fun of Walking the Streets

The fun of walking around a Chinese city is that so much life takes place out on the streets. In a developed nation like the U.S., most life takes place behind closed doors. In a society steeped in history and tradition like China, much more happens right out in the open—that's simply the way it's been

for centuries. For one thing, most Chinese still don't own a car. They walk or take a bicycle or a bus to where they need to go, instead of each being encased in their own little bubble, out of touch with other people. For another, Chinese homes and apartments are much smaller than those in developed countries. Activities like washing clothes or cleaning vegetables, reading the newspaper, or even brushing one's teeth are often done right out in public in full view of passersby.

One more big reason why so much of daily life can be glimpsed outdoors is that in China there have been as many as two hundred million people who left their homes in small towns or the countryside to try to make a better life in the large cities. That means there is a sizeable population in every major Chinese city without any fixed abode. They eat, play cards and chess, and carry on their daily life totally on the streets. In addition, Chinese cities are a giant collection of a myriad small shops and vendors' stalls and eateries that are often right on the street or with their storefront totally open to the street. Beyond going to the major tourist sites in any Chinese city, it behooves any foreign tourist to wander the streets and see how the Chinese really live. It's a feast for the senses and a photographer's delight.

There are two problems that a foreigner faces, however, when walking the streets of a Chinese city that one does not encounter in a country like the U.S. Neither has to do with personal safety. As we keep insisting, you are much safer walking the streets of Beijing or Shanghai, even at midnight, than you are walking in midday in your hometown in the U.S., whether that town is New York City or Pella, Iowa. No one has guns, the police are everywhere, albeit often undercover, and serious crime is still a fraction of what it is in America. No, the two problems you face are ones for which most Americans are unprepared.

People, People, Everywhere!

The first difficulty in walking down the street in China is the sea of humanity through which you must wade in order to get where you're going. Unless you spend a good deal of time in downtown Manhattan or Chicago, chances are you aren't used to walking much. And when you do walk, you're used to being able to walk pretty much as fast as you'd like. In a Chinese city you have to learn to slow your pace because there will always be hundreds of people in front of you, behind you, and alongside of you.

Imagine the most popular store in your hometown the day before Christmas, when shoppers are knocking each oth-

er over to get to grab last minute presents for friends and family. Now picture the density of people at a hundred times that of the store on Christmas Eve. Finally multiply the number of people by ten thousand. Place them out on the main street of your hometown and imagine them all trying to get somewhere at the same time. You now have some idea of what it's like on a typical Chinese city street at almost any time of the day or night. You're just not going to get anywhere very fast. The only way for you and your companion to walk side by side is for you to do what the Chinese do, which is to hold each other tightly by the hand or, preferably, link arms.

The crowded streets of Chinese cities, however, are only a minor inconvenience compared to the other problem faced by tourists when walking around a Chinese city. This is a problem that endangers your life almost every minute. We refer, of course, to crossing the street. Here you are taking your life in your hands unless you realize that the Chinese operate under a completely different set of rules when it comes to things like "right of way." Crossing the street in China requires the watchfulness of an eagle, the agility of a mountain lion, the guile of a fox, and the luck of the Irish to make it across safely. If, however, you pay attention to the simple rules below, you may make it across the street and live to tell about it. Skip this section and you may end up spending the rest of your China trip learning more than you ever wanted to know about Chinese hospitals.

Crossing the Street

In the U.S. the pedestrian has the right of way. When the walk light comes on, the pedestrian may usually safely cross the street, checking briefly to see that all traffic has come to a halt. In China the pedestrian NEVER has the right of way. In fact, the right of way goes to the biggest and fastest vehicle. There's no written law that states this. Everyone just seems to understand. It's simple logic, really. Big trucks and buses take right of way over smaller buses, which lord it over taxis, which bully private cars. Taxis hold sway over other cars because owners of private autos don't want to damage their shiny new treasure, whereas most taxi drivers in China seem to have definite suicidal tendencies more akin to those of "kamikaze" pilots. Any motorized vehicle, including motorcycles, has the right of way over bicycles, whose riders will not hesitate to run over a pedestrian who dares question the vehicular pecking order by walking in front of them. While most vehicles do obey the stop and go lights, the millions of bicycle riders in China never worry about a little thing like a traffic light. Those, it seems, are just for cars and buses. Bicyclists may cross your path whether you have the walk light or not. The pedestrian is the low man or woman on the totem pole of Chinese traffic, the lowest link on the transportation evolutionary scale. Crossing a street is like playing a real life game of "Frogger."

How to cross the road when there are mad bicyclists coming at you from every direction and a constant stream of cars and buses? Learn from herds of wildebeests or antelope in the Serengeti. They know there is safety in numbers. Those that stray from the herd are the ones that usually end up getting eaten. So do what the Chinese do: Never cross the street alone, or even in pairs. Wait for a small group of local Chinese people who want to cross the street in the same direction you wish to go. Position yourself, if possible, in the middle of this pack of people. Watch for them to make their move and then go with them.

What can happen when a lone foreign pedestrian bravely tries to cross the street on his own? Let us give you the sad example of Larry when he tried to lead the way across a street in downtown Shanghai at rush hour. Having located a crosswalk, albeit with no walk light, he started across the street, constantly looking left and right for oncoming vehicles. There was such a pile of cars and buses that traffic had come to a standstill. It seemed like an easy task to make it across. When he had reached the middle of the street, he turned and took a step back to beckon for Qin to follow him. Just then a young woman on a bicycle came out of nowhere and ran right over his foot. The bicyclist had precisely planned her move through the thick traffic based on Larry continuing to walk forward. But Larry crossed her up by turning back. He fell hard on the pavement, scraping both of his knees, which were bleeding profusely. Later that day he realized that his foot was broken and that it had to be set in a cast, which ended the trip a week early.

Encountering Beggars

At this point remove your funny bone and set it aside. We need to talk a bit about begging and it's hard to find any humor in the misery of others. When you walk the streets of most countries in the world you will encounter beggars. In many developing countries you will sometimes be mobbed by them. Even in the U.S. we have people begging, and in a comparatively economically poorer nation like India or China you expect to see a lot more of it. When you consider how wealthy we Americans are compared to most people in the world, it's only natural that the impoverished in developing countries might expect us to toss a few coins their way. The problem is more and more people are thinking this way, and many Chinese cities have become magnets for a wave of human misery, and, sadly, those who profit from it. There is no point in ignoring it since you will not be able to avoid seeing these people on the street, but it's best to understand as much as you can before seeing any unpleasant surprises.

China is doing a whole lot better economically than most

other developing nations. There has been a tremendous rise in the standard of living for a large percentage of Chinese in the past few decades. Part of China's economic miracle in the past 25 years is that the country has managed to move 300 million people out of poverty and quadruple the average person's income in less than one generation. Nevertheless, the average yearly income of a Chinese person today is still only around U.S. $1,000 compared to around $30,000 for the average American. But that's just the average Chinese income. There are huge, even staggering, gaps in wealth—stark reminders of China's free-for-all economy that is churning out more millionaires at a breakneck pace.

Since China has the greatest disparity of wealth of any nation now, a large number of Chinese live on the equivalent of only a few hundred U.S. dollars per year. Most Chinese do think of all Americans as wealthy. After all, we had the money to fly halfway around the world to make it to China, so you figure that at least some Chinese will view us foreign tourists as walking wallets and ask for a handout.

Actually, one of the impressive things about China is that, relatively speaking, there are so few people begging in the streets compared to most other developing nations. Most of the 1.3 billion Chinese people have adequate shelter, food, and clothing. You really won't be accosted in China by a great number of people begging. But they are there and you need to be prepared. Beggars in China may not be many, but there are quite a variety of them.

You might be approached by a young boy of five with dirty face and tattered clothing, who will follow you around with his hand out. Or there might be an elderly woman who seizes you by the arm and won't let go, expecting you to give her money. Or you may see someone with his legs bent under him in shabby clothing sitting in the middle of the walkway with a cup in front of him, prostrating himself to passersby on a piece of cardboard.

It's not easy at first to pass these people by. Most of us have good hearts. It's also obvious how rich we are compared to them. The crippled people really pull at your heartstrings, and seeing children in such a state can be deeply troubling. What's even worse is that many children have been deliberately maimed or disfigured by adults, who realized that they can make more money by using a child to beg for them. As hard as it may be, do not give them money.

In front of our hotel in the heart of the city of Xian, for example, there is a relatively healthy-looking boy of around five or six years old whose daily job it is to work the front of the hotel. He approaches every foreign tourist with his palm out. If you ignore him, he will follow you for a distance tugging at your sleeve. Meanwhile his mother works a block or so down the same street. Her job is to kneel in front of pass-ersby with her youngest son and ask for money. But come noon, we have seen that mother gather up her two children and take them to McDonald's. They are an attractive family, who look healthy and well fed. The only pitiful things about them are the smudged faces of the children and the dirtied clothing they wear.

For those who exploit children, making them do the begging work while they collect the proceeds, giving them money only makes the situation worse when you look at the big picture. It is hard to think of it in this way, but this is the reality. Try not to look at beggars or engage them in conver-sation. Rather, give them a wide berth when walking down the street. If one of them takes a hold of your arm, gently but firmly push it away and walk on with a determined gait. This is no time to practice speaking Chinese with the locals. Again, do not give them money, as hard as it may be. Give your money instead to an international charity or a local branch of a charity you know and can trust to help people who are in need.

Spitting in the Streets

Less than ideal sanitary conditions in China still make con-gestion of the lungs and throat an endemic problem for many Chinese. Another reason for all the coughing and hacking you hear may just have to do with the fact that over

60% of Chinese men smoke like chimneys. The traditional solution for getting rid of that nasty mucus build-up is by spitting it out on the street. This creates a number of little puddles that you will want to avoid. It's a bit like walking gingerly through a minefield, being careful to watch where you step. You must also keep your ears on the alert for the sound of someone about to "hawk." Much as the mosquito buzzes or the rattlesnake rattles before striking, the "hawker" first has to go into his wind-up before the pitch. The warning sound of someone collecting the phlegm in his throat is a lot like the sound "hur" as in the word "hurl." When you hear this sound, quickly move as far away as you can from the source of the sound. For men, if you are standing at a urinal and a Chinese man comes up to the urinal next to you, there is a 99% chance he is going to hawk and clear his throat, while taking care of business, in which case the sound will echo mercilessly off the bathroom walls.

If you can read Chinese, you know from your first day in China that spitting is a common phenomenon. Why else would there be signs everywhere telling you not to just spit on the streets as you please. In spite of the tremendous gains in literacy in China over the past few decades, some-how people don't seem to be able to read the characters for "spitting!" We'd suggest those characters be taught in the first grade!

The time of year when the spit really flies is the winter. The cheap grade of coal the Chinese use for heating and in-dustry helps make bronchial colds as common as sunburn at a nudist colony. If you're in China in the heat of summer, consider yourself lucky that the wetness you feel on your neck is only from your own perspiration!

If you had visited China several decades earlier, there would have been an additional kind of minefield you would have had to walk through on the streets. Those were the puddles left by toddlers who had relieved themselves as the need arose. Chinese tradition has always encouraged par-ents to wait longer to toilet train their young children than we do in America. Rather than putting a diaper on their youngster, Chinese parents will traditionally give them a pair of trousers with a slit down the middle. When the child feels the urge to go, he or she only needs to squat down and the pants will split wide open. For centuries this strategy worked just fine in the fields, where the youngsters would help fertilize the crops. On crowded city sidewalks, how-ever, this isn't such a great idea. When the peasants started streaming into the cities in the early 1980s seeking a better life, it took a while for them to be convinced that the split pants were not welcome in downtown Beijing or Shanghai.

Hardships for the Handicapped

If an ordinary tourist feels handicapped by so many obstacles on a Chinese street, it is even harder for truly handicapped people. As in most developing countries, there are few places with accommodations for the disabled. There is too little public money and too little awareness to build such facilities. In museums, palaces, parks, temples, churches, etc., there are rarely any ramps for wheelchairs, for example. In addition, Chinese architectural tradition dictates the necessity of very high thresholds that you must walk over to enter any home or temple. This high threshold is to prevent evil spirits from entering. It also proves a true barrier for the handicapped. Add to that the Chinese predilection for long stone staircases leading to the inner sanctum of ancient temples as well as up the hillsides to even reach the temples, and you have a truly difficult scenario for anyone getting around in a wheelchair.

Public restrooms never make provisions for the handicapped. In many airport washrooms, for example, there are not one but two steps up to enter! For all these reasons it is rare to see any handicapped Chinese people venture out to many historic sites.

There is one more obstacle for handicapped and non-handicapped people alike that you should be forewarned about. This is the very common practice in most Chinese hotels of building the bathroom a half step lower than the rest of the hotel room. This means that you must always be prepared to step down into the washroom. Foreign tourists who are used to hotel bathrooms and bedrooms being on the same level are almost always surprised when they take that first step.

Essentials for Walking

Besides carrying some water with you as you wander through the streets of a Chinese city, it is highly suggested that you also have with you at all times the following equipment:

Earplugs will be necessary to defend yourself from all the noise pollution you will encounter in a typical Chinese city. There is, of course, the constant stream of traffic that is a wondrous mix of buses, trucks, cars, taxis, motorcycles, and sometimes donkey-drawn carts. All of these vehicles, except the donkey carts, are equipped with horns. The Chinese driver would not be able to drive without constantly sounding the horn. It seems that in the driver's training manual in China the words for "clutch" and "horn" were inadvertently switched. The constant sounding of the horn by the Chinese driver alerts the thousands of people around him that he's in the vicinity and they better get out of his way if they know what's good for them. Unfortunately, since everyone is trying to pass everyone else ALL the time, everyone is always sounding his horn. We recommend industrial-strength earplugs with a minimal rating of 100 decibels. Then let the horns blare away.

Another reason for the earplugs is the quaint Chinese

custom regarding garbage trucks. In China there are a lot of people. Those people produce a lot of garbage. Some-one needs to be con-stantly removing that gar-

bage. So the trucks come around at all hours to pick up the trash in the different neighborhoods. There's no place for dumpsters in most of China. The store and restaurant own-ers in shopping areas, for instance, have to bring their trash out to the truck when it drives by. In order to alert everyone to the fact that the garbage truck has arrived, the trucks are programmed to play a tune very loudly to announce their presence. It's a lot like the Good Humor ice cream truck that still comes to our suburban neighborhood in Michigan. But instead of carrying a yummy chocolate fudge bar, it's there to pick up your trash. And instead of playing something really rousing and lovely, like "Popeye the Sailorman," it plays something really annoying like "Rubber Ducky!"

Right in front of our hotel in the picturesque ancient mountain village of Dali, a garbage truck came by every day in the late afternoon to serenade us with "Happy Birthday to You" over and over and over again. The truck usually stayed there for five very slow minutes, blaring out "Happy Birthday to You" as if it were the Chinese National Anthem and this was "National Day" in China. Without earplugs we would surely have strangled the driver. Our earplugs definitely kept us from being involved in an international incident that would have included some major jail time.

If you intend to go to one of the many spectacularly scenic mountain areas where the elevation is more than a mile above sea level, you may seriously want to think about supplementary oxygen, as crazy as it may sound. You may not actually need to carry it, but it pays to know where you can get it. When we traveled recently to the high mountains of Sichuan, near the border with Tibet, Qin suddenly felt a shortness of breath. Now Qin has yet to reach the age that the Chinese call "half a hundred." She's also slim and walks many miles a day back in her adopted homeland of Michigan. But there she was, having trouble just taking a breath. Larry rushed to the local hospital where he was given an oxygen pillow with a breathing tube attached. This served as Qin's lifeline for the next several days.

Shop till You Drop

When visiting any major tourist attraction in China, you will need to run the gauntlet of numerous street vendors. These appear to have been ingeniously set up and placed in strategic locations for the sole purpose of enticing foreign shoppers.

Many of these vendors have stalls set up on either side of the narrow street leading to a famous temple or historic site. These professional salespeople are selling every conceivable kind of souvenir, from painted fans and painted scrolls to battery-powered pandas and Tibetan hats. They appear to be under strict instructions from the government to not allow any tourists to pass without trying to get them to enter their open-air shop. As you walk by you will be assailed with cries of "haroo, haroo" or "just looking, just looking." Somehow they have picked up on English-speaking tourists insisting that they were "just looking," and have twisted it around to mean "come in for a look and spend a pleasant hour or two admiring our merchandise." Should you stop to gaze at some picture postcards or a fake Tang dynasty clay horse, they will be all over you like hair on a gorilla. The Chinese vendor immediately smells a sale. He or she quickly and silently slithers over to you to close in for the kill.

There are some simple rules to follow:

- Only stop at a stall or open-air shop where there are some tchotchkies of real interest.
- Do not look the vendors in the eyes but continue to stare at the item. Otherwise, like a snake charmer, they will start to weave their spell on you. They will tell you about the amazing qualities of the item, who made it, how many generations of artisans it took to perfect this craft, and why you should purchase at least two.
- If you are interested in a particular souvenir item, never accept the price they offer. Always try offering the vendor ⅕ to ¹⁄₁₀ of their price as your starting offer. Almost everything that's for sale in China has a price that's negotiable.

How to Bargain

You can haggle over the price for just about everything in China. It's a game that all Chinese play when they shop at a store or a vendor's stall. If you as a foreign tourist don't play the game, they think of you as a real chump. If you end up paying anything close to the original asking price, you've been had. It's as if every shop in China is like your

local car dealer. Your average car salesman asks you to pay $16,000 for a Honda Civic, knowing that you will eventually haggle the price down to $14,000 and get him to throw in a free keyless remote and a free CD player. But imagine if the car dealership had a sticker price of $80,000 for that Honda Civic, expecting you to be smart enough to know that it should really go for $14,000 with the keyless remote and CD player added for good measure. Now imagine that just about every store in America was like a car dealership. The sticker price is only a starting point for a heated negotiation between the salesperson and the customer over the final price of the item. You then have a picture of what it's like to shop in China. There are some major exceptions where haggling is not allowed, such as in hotels, restaurants, supermarkets, bookstores, and pharmacies.

In most other places of business, however, from giant electronic stores to small shops and street stalls, bargaining over the price is fair game.

Here's how the game is played. You see an embroidered silk jacket that you like. You innocently ask the price. If you were Chinese, the shopkeeper or vendor might ask for 30 yuan. Seeing your foreign face, however, which looks to

them like a giant dollar sign with a mouth, they ask you for 200 yuan. A Chinese person would know from experience what a certain kind of item is probably worth and offer to pay a little less than that. You as a foreigner have no idea. 200 yuan is only approximately U.S. $25, so it actually seems like a good deal. Wow, this may be a real bargain and you hand over the 200 yuan. Man, did you blow it! It's not just that you have paid six or seven times what the item should have sold for, you have actually encouraged the vendor to continue to jack up the price of things for foreigners.

The Chinese merchant will be all the more likely to eye greedily any tourist who walks by his shop in the same way a spider views a fly, or a cat views a mouse, or a political canvasser views an open door.

Here is the way the Chinese would purchase the em- broidered silk jacket. You should follow their example. Since most things in China are usually not one of a kind, but available from countless other shops or stalls in that same neighborhood—often a few feet away—never buy anything without comparative shopping. See what other vendors will ask for that same jacket. The first vendor asked you for 200 yuan, but at another shop you see the same jacket and they ask you for 100 yuan. In a third shop you overhear the shop-keeper offer the exact same jacket to a Chinese tourist for 80 and the Chinese ends up paying only 25 yuan. Then you know what the going price should really be.

Below is a sample conversation between a Chinese shop-keeper and a savvy tourist:

Shopkeeper: You like that painting? It's by very famous local artist. Very beautiful.
Tourist: How much?
Shopkeeper (after a contemplative pause, for added effect): I give it to you for 200 yuan.
Tourist: That's way too expensive. How about 50 yuan?
Shopkeeper: 50 yuan?! (Shaking his head and laughing) No, no, way too little. How about 150 yuan?
Tourist: That's way too much. Forget it! (starts to walk away)
Shopkeeper: O.K., O.K. To make a friend, only 50 yuan.
Tourist: 40.
Shopkeeper: O.K., O.K., only 40.

Enjoy the game. The shopkeepers and vendors will respect you more if you haggle with them. It's a way of life. Some foreigners don't like the hassle of always bargaining for every souvenir. It can get pretty tiring after a while. The truth is that pretty soon you will get used to the pricing system and bargaining actually becomes easier. Some of our students actually claim they miss it when they return home, where they're tempted to bargain down the price of Pop Tarts with the cashier in the checkout lane of their local supermarket!

The Aggressive Vendor

Of all the obstacles the tourist faces on a Chinese city street, perhaps the most troublesome and the most annoying is the aggressive itinerant vendor. Not all people who are trying to sell you things in China have their own shop or market stall. Many are small-scale sellers with only a few choice souvenir items they want to foist on tourists. They congregate around the famous tourist sites waiting for their chance to pounce. This is a true cat and mouse game, and you're the mouse!

Let's say you go to see the world famous tomb of the Qin (pronounced "chin") Emperor. You spend a few hours alongside hundreds of other tourists gawking at the nearly seven thousand terra cotta soldiers that have guarded this tomb for more than two thousand years. It's time to head back to the hotel. You have that satisfied feeling that indeed your trip to China has been worth it. For you have seen what the Chinese claim is the eighth man-made wonder of the world and it was spectacular. You have gotten a glimpse of what the army of the first emperor of China looked like. You have stepped back in time.

Feeling at peace with the world, you exit the museum area and begin walking back to where you can board your waiting bus or taxi. What you haven't been prepared for is a living army of itinerant vendors from the countryside. Each is armed with a single small box that contains exactly the same thing—four small replicas of the terra cotta warriors and their horses. You make the mistake of casually looking inside one of the boxes as you pass the first vendor. It is then that he begins his cry of "one dallah, one dallah" (English translation: "one dollar," i.e. "going cheap"). You hurry by the first vendor only to be accosted by a second . . . and a third and a fourth. You walk faster now, trying not to look at the other vendors. They hurry after you, thrusting their box in front of you to give you a close look at the bargain they're offering you. Shouting "no, no" or, if you know Chinese, "bú yào, bú yào" (boo yow, boo yow = not want, not want), you try to hurry by. Breaking into a slow trot you make it to within sight of the parking lot. You're home-free now, you think. You breathe a sigh of relief.

Suddenly you see in front of you a group of vendors blocking your way, making a last ditch stand to prevent you from leaving the tourist site without buying something useless. The most aggressive of the pack follows alongside you for 20 or 30 paces. He grabs your arm, insisting that you cannot live without four small clay warriors in a box. You tell him you wouldn't want his box of bric-a-brac even if it were free. He presses you all the more closely until you tell him to shove off. He curses you in Chinese and finally heads off to harass another victim.

You have just witnessed one of the downsides of the new

capitalism in China. For the first three decades of Communist rule little free enterprise was allowed. Now that almost anything can be sold freely in China, every peasant and his grandmother seems to be out on the street trying to make a fast buck. The Chinese slogan has changed from Mao's "Serve the people" to Deng Xiaoping's "Suck people dry." O.K., the famous quote attributed to Deng is really "To get rich is glorious." But "suck people dry" is the phrase that's caught on, it appears. You begin to miss the days when all Chinese wore Mao jackets and the only things for sale on the street were Popsicles or watermelon. Now that there is an army of vendors on the march in China, trying to sell you anything they can get their hands on, how is the lone tourist to face such an assault?

Shopping in Large Stores

Say you decide to take refuge from the aggressive street vendors by shopping in a department store. Or you'd like to buy something from a large bookstore or pharmacy.

In these kinds of stores the sales people are far less aggressive than the small shop owners or street vendors. That's because they're not the owners but only employees and often don't care that much whether you buy something or not. They're also behind counters, so they can't easily seize you by the arm. You figure you're safe now and it'll be just like shopping in a large store in America.

You'd be right except for one thing. The way you pay

for things. In every larger store in China except for supermarkets the Chinese have made the process of paying for what you'd like to buy as complicated and

as time-consuming as possible. Say you go to a department store. On the first floor you find a lovely pair of earrings in the shape of panda bears. You decide that they're a bargain at 80 yuan (around U.S.$10). You hold out 80 yuan to the store clerk, but instead of giving you the earrings, she gives you a bill for the earrings and motions for you to go thirty feet away to a cashier's counter. It's there that you have to "wait in line" to pay for your earrings and get a receipt. You then take the receipt back to the clerk who will finally hand over the earrings. It seems that the store doesn't feel that you can trust one person to both handle the merchandise and handle money, too. No, those are separate jobs, each of which requires someone with specialized expertise. In our family, for instance, Qin is good at handling money while Larry is only good at taking things down off shelves. Hmm, maybe the Chinese have a point after all!

Anyway, just in making one purchase you get in some pretty good exercise running back and forth between the counter with the merchandise, the cashier's stand, and back

to the counter again. If you find a pair of swim fins on the second floor, you'll have to go through the same thing all over again on the second floor that you went through on the first. Swim fins are a different section of the store and you must pay for each item at the cashier's stand in each separate department. If you buy one item on all six floors of the department store you will have run pretty much the equivalent of a marathon by the time you've completed all your purchases.

This system is aggravating enough if you're completely sound of limb. The time it became almost too much to bear was when Larry was hit by that bicyclist in Shanghai and his foot was broken. He also had numerous cuts and bruises on his knees and legs, which were bleeding profusely. He hobbled into a pharmacy nearby, where he was told he needed to go up to the second floor for disinfectant and bandages. Since the pharmacy was one of the older government-run businesses, there was no elevator or escalator. It took him five minutes of excruciating pain to hop on one foot up the long staircase to the second floor. It was comical and pathetic at the same time. He asked for disinfectant and bandages, along with some tape to hold the bandages. The clerks took the things off the shelves, but since this was China they couldn't give him the merchandise.

Instead they handed him the various charge slips for the three purchases and pointed to the cashier's desk. It was all the way across the floor from the counter where he was leaning. Dragging his broken foot behind him it took him what seemed another five minutes to hobble over to the cashier, pay for the items, and then return to where the supplies he needed were waiting for him. What made things worse was that the temperature that day was around 95 degrees, with a humidity of at least 101%. And there was neither air conditioning on the second floor of the store nor a fan nor even a single window.

To be fair, it was then that Larry was reminded of how very nice the Chinese can often be to foreigners. They're not always trying to rip us off. Several of the women clerks in the pharmacy finally took pity on the sweating, bleeding, hobbling middle-aged American. They put Larry in a room nearby, sat him down, turned on a fan, and set to disinfecting and bandaging his wounds themselves as if this were a hospital rather than a drugstore. These ladies not only soothed the physical wounds that Larry had suffered. They also helped heal the wounds to the spirit he had felt by the bicyclist who had not stopped when she knocked him over in the street.

7

Medical Emergencies

Given the various dangers that China presents, from kamikaze bikers and taxi drivers to food to which western stomachs are not accustomed and viruses to which westerners have never been exposed, you may find yourself needing some medical care during your time in the Middle Kingdom. Do not despair. Help for anything that ails you is definitely available.

If it's a mere cold or cough that you develop, you will find drugstores on many a major street. In the largest cities like Beijing and Shanghai you can find a western pharmacy with everything from aspirin to Tylenol and Advil. In smaller cities, however, the pharmacies will carry Chinese brands of these same medicines, with lovely Chinese characters decorating the entire box or package. If you don't speak or read Chinese, not to worry. Simply act out your symptoms, such as sneezing or coughing all over the drug store clerk. They'll soon get the idea as to what is troubling you, and rush to grab the appropriate antidote. Should they rush to the back room and not return after a half hour, you can safely assume they have been thoroughly grossed out by your overly effusive impression of a tubercular patient, and have retired for safety to the inner sanctum of the store. But if you don't overdo your demonstration, most likely they will hand over the preferred medication for your ailment.

Be aware, however, that in China there are two very different systems of medical treatments that are provided. One is the "modern," or "western" one with which foreigners are familiar. The other system is that of traditional Chinese medicine, which uses acupuncture, moxibustion, and time-honored herbal remedies, instead of western medicines, to treat various conditions. Each hospital has a wing devoted to western medicine and another to traditional Chinese treatments. The same is true of the largest pharmacies. But in most cities in China pharmacies devote themselves to either one or the other system of treatment. If you simply ask someone to direct you to a nearby pharmacy or you see a store that looks like it might carry medicines with clerks in white uniforms, you may find yourself in a shop with drawer after drawer of herbs, berries, and deer antlers. So be sure to ask not just for a "yàofáng" (yowfahng) or "pharmacy," but a "xī yàofáng" (see yowfahng) or "western-style pharmacy" if it's aspirin or Tylenol you're looking for.

If you develop a really serious condition, such as a having a heart attack upon seeing your hotel bill which includes all those little bottles of alcohol that you thought were complimentary but which were priced at 300 yuan per bottle, then the good folks at the front desk of the hotel will arrange for an ambulance to come and whisk you away to the nearest hospital that handles foreign guests.

If, however, the medical problem you develop is neither rather minor nor extremely serious, but is somewhere in the gray area between a head cold and a heart attack, then there are certain things of which you should be aware.

First of all, pretty much any large hotel in China has a small medical staff on hand to help you with problems that can be treated on an out-patient basis. If you need a wound bandaged or an ingrown toenail attended to, refer to the hotel guide in your room or call the front desk and ask the location of the small clinic in the hotel.

The average hotel in China, however, lacks such a clinic. But the larger cities of China do have at least one hospital that is their very best and that has a special section devoted to treating foreign guests. Often these are referred to as "Number 1" hospitals. Western guests are not used to waiting in long lines all day at the hospital before they get to finally see a doctor. The Chinese, being aware of this and wanting to keep the tourist dollars flowing by providing speedier service for foreigners, have a small part of some of their hospitals ready to serve us, who will pay what to the Chinese are devilishly high prices for special medical care given by doctors who speak English.

Larry and Qin did not realize the above fact, however,

and when Larry had his foot broken in Shanghai, the hotel clinic did not have an x-ray machine, nor could they give Larry a cast for his foot. They did, however,

give us the name and address of the hotel that serves foreigners, and off we went in a cab to that location.

The taxi took us to the front entrance of the hospital, where we got out only to encounter a swarm of Chinese people outside the front door waiting to get in to see a doctor. Despairing of ever seeing a doctor that day or even that week, some thoughtful Chinese person pointed out to us that the entrance for foreigners was by another door. All we had to do was walk a block down the street, turn and walk another block, and we would find that special back entrance. The only problem was that Larry's foot was broken and he had no crutches. So here was this image of a pathetic, lame, middle-aged man with what appeared to be a clubfoot, dragged his aching body several blocks to the door by which foreigners are allowed to enter the hospital.

Once inside there was only a short wait before Larry was seen by a most competent doctor who, it was said, spoke some limited English but with whom we opted to speak his native language of Chinese. The good doctor told Larry that his foot needed to be x-rayed before he treated it. In came a thin man in his fifties pushing a wheelchair, who then proceeded to push Larry the two or three miles (or so it seemed) to the x-ray room in the Chinese part of the hospital. Larry's wheelchair was pushed past hundreds of Chinese people of all ages waiting in the hallway, then pushed ahead of all the Chinese waiting for x-rays, to come to a stop before a large x-ray machine that looked like it had been the top of the line—in the 1930s! But he didn't need to wait for hours for his x-ray, like all those Chinese people who had made their way to the hospital at the crack of dawn. Larry was treated like an honored foreign guest.

The x-ray machine confirmed that Larry indeed had a broken foot. The Chinese technician, on seeing Larry's foot, couldn't help from exclaiming: "What a big foot!" which, of course, made Larry feel so much better. It was another exhilarating ride in the wheelchair past hundreds of pairs of curious eyes as he was escorted back to the waiting doctor. The Chinese physician, with the help of a nurse, began to make a plaster cast in which to mummify Larry's foot. Only when Larry returned home to a specialist in Michigan did he discover that an American doctor would have instead given him a lightweight boot to wear on his foot, one that could be removed every evening so he could bathe. Instead Larry's foot looked like an appendage of King Tut, except that the bandages were whiter. And for only $10 or so he

got a lovely pair of crutches to allow him to walk around and show off his new cast to the entire population of Shanghai. In this kind of upscale hospital with a specialty section for foreigners, you may pay by either credit card or cash. Upon returning home you can then send the receipt to your insurance company and be reimbursed for whatever is covered by your policy.

The upshot of this story is that you should make sure you find out whether the hospital to which you go for treatment has a special section for foreigners, and then have your taxi driver drop you in front of that entrance.

There is another important piece of information that you need to know regarding medical emergencies. You may have to go a hospital in China to simply get some medical device or piece of equipment that is not available in a pharmacy. Crutches, for instance. Or an oxygen tank! Take the case of Qin when she was with Larry in the town of Lijiang, set picturesquely in the mountains of the southwestern province of Yunnan, near Tibet. The altitude of the town is around 2,800 meters or roughly 8,400 feet. Unfortunately it turned out that Qin's body could not adapt to the high altitude. The

Chinese refer to people who can't swim or who don't like water as "hàn yāzi" or "dry-land duck." It seems that Qin was a "dīdì yāzi," or "low-land duck."

After a day walking around the mountains at nosebleed height, Qin was really having trouble breathing and was in need of supplementary oxygen.

Larry commandeered a taxi to take him to the nearest hospital to get some kind of oxygen tank. Fortunately the driver, who was a chronologically gifted and kind man, had already guessed that Larry was unfamiliar with the procedure for obtaining an oxygen tank in a regular Chinese hospital, and actually went into the hospital with Larry to help. He first asked the way to the place where he could get Larry a portable supply of oxygen, asked the name of the piece of equipment, then went to a different part of the hospital where Larry had to pay first, then took the receipt from him back to the original place to obtain the oxygen. What they gave him, by the way, was a large flat pillow that seemed to be of no use in this emergency. But the hospital staff then proceeded to fill the pillow with oxygen and showed Larry that there was a tube attached to the pillow which could then be attached to the patient's nose. It was through this that Qin could inhale the extra dose of oxygen she needed back in the hotel room. If you are not so fortunate as to have a compassionate cab driver to help you, make sure you are aware of the system in Chinese hospitals: "Pay first, get your respirator later."

In case you should have the misfortune to need medical attention someplace in China outside of the major cities, then you should be aware of the following: The only way to see a doctor or to get a prescription in China is to go a hospital.

Doctors do not have separate offices as they do here in the U.S. Chinese hospitals are classified into four different levels in a hierarchy of quality and scope of medical care. So-called "international" hospitals like the Beijing Hospital are few in number and can only be found in Beijing. These are the top of the line. They are open to the general Chinese public, but the finest physicians and facilities are reserved for a section of the hospital open only to high Party officials and, of course, to foreigners.

The second tier of hospitals is that of the "city hospital." These offer care on a level that would be acceptable to foreigners. Such hospitals treat ordinary Chinese for surgeries and x-rays, and are well-run with decent equipment. This is the place for foreigners to go if they're not in Beijing, and it was to such a hospital to which Larry hobbled on his broken foot.

The third grade of hospital is the "district hospital." This is where Chinese go for treatment of common ailments like a cold, the flu, stomach troubles, cuts, and the like.

No surgical operations are performed here, but they feature both Chinese and western medicines and also offer massage therapy and acupuncture treatment. This is definitely the cheapest place to go for a good massage, not only

in China but in most of the world.

The fourth and lowest level of medical care is provided by the small neighborhood or rural clinic. These are often just a few rooms in a shabby one-story building. It's sufficient for first-aid and basic medical advice, and also allows Chinese in the neighborhood to renew and fill their prescriptions without having to make the trek to a large hospital.

If you are a foreigner and develop a medical problem, then it's best to have your problem in Beijing. Otherwise go to a "city hospital," called "shìjí yīyuàn" (shure-jee-ee-yuen). Often the specific hospital of this type will have the words "rénmín" or "people's" hospital in the title. When you visit a regular hospital in China that does not have a section specifically reserved for foreigners, you will feel like you're in that interminable line of Chinese people as you wade through what seems to be the entire population of China just to get into the front door of the hospital.

For some, the size of the crowds can be intimidating beyond words. If you find yourself in a facility where you can only receive the same kind of treatment that the ordinary Chinese person receives when needing medical care, don't give up completely. It may seem ridiculously complicated, frustratingly slow, and full of humiliation, but it will only cost you time. Given the choice between seeing someone—anyone, and going it alone, we would argue that waiting for medical care is better than not waiting for it.

When you visit a Chinese hospital the first thing you do is to register or "guàhào" (gwah-how) in the Lobby, right inside the front door. The front door opens at 7:30 A.M., by which time the crowd of people who have been waiting outside since 5:00 or 5:30 that morning have already formed a long line ahead of you.

When you finally get into the Lobby you will see several windows on each side.

If you're not sure which window is for registration, simply get in the longest line, because that's definitely the line for registration. When you finally make your way to the front of the line, you will pay a small amount of money to register, ten or twenty yuan, for which you receive a tiny, flimsy slip of paper with a number on it. Guard that little piece of paper as you would the most precious thing in the world, as this paper is the only proof you have that you registered for that day. You will need to figure out for yourself which department you need to register for, depending on your condition, from general internal medicine to osteopathy to gynecology to surgery.

Now you have to find out where in the hospital that department for which you registered might be hidden. When you find the right department you will usually see a desk in the front room, behind which sits a very stern-looking young or middle-aged woman in a white uniform. Do not wrongly assume that this person, who works in a hospital, knows anything about medicine or has any sense of concern for the welfare of sick people. You duly hand over your flimsy slip of paper with your number on it to that lady. If you have been a patient in that hospital before, you also offer up your little booklet with your medical history, called a "bìnglì" (bing-lee). If this is your first visit to the hospital, you'll need to purchase a little blank booklet when you register.

Then you wait. Often there's no seat. Usually a hundred people are waiting there, sneezing, coughing, moaning, lying on benches or crouched on the floor. The last thing you want to do is wait there with them, because you're pretty sure that you would then be exposed to at least a dozen diseases that are all much worse than what you have. You want to go somewhere else, anywhere else, to wait. But you would be making a BIG mistake. That's because there is no way to know which "number" the doctor is seeing at that time, so you have to constantly ask the stern-faced dragon lady at the desk how things are progressing. If you should leave and your number is called while you're away, you're in for a good tongue-lashing from Mrs. Dragon Lady upon your return. You will definitely not be next in line, but will possibly be punished by being put at the end of the line. At the very least several other patients will be allowed to go ahead of you.

Finally your long wait to see a doctor is rewarded. Your number is called. You press through the waiting throng into the doctor's office, only to discover

that there are at least two doctors, and sometimes three or four, occupying the same small office. The doctors have their desks placed facing one another, which seems very friendly and a most economical use of space. It also means, however, that you sit on one side of the doctor and, sitting a foot or two away from you is another patient sitting alongside the other doctor. And the other patient may have his or her entire family, including all his or her cousins, standing there to lend moral support. So if you should have a severe itch in the groin or a bad case of 'roids, you may decide to not tell the doctor your problem, lest everyone else in the room learn about your diagnosis. And the door to the doctor's office is never closed. There are always many people waiting at the entrance to get in. So you may have an audience of a few dozen people, seemingly all with their eyes fixed on you, waiting to hear what the foreigner has wrong with him.

So let's say that the doctor needs to examine you. You go to one side of the room. There's an examining table in a corner, onto which you hop. The doctor courteously draws a flimsy curtain around you to give you privacy. But there are still a dozen people right outside the curtain who can hear everything that's said.

Let's say you've endured this humiliation. You emerge, facing all the staring eyes fixed on you. The physician now says that he or she needs a sample of skin or blood, depending on your ailment. Or you have a stomach complaint and they need a urine or stool sample. The doctor then writes out something on another little flimsy piece of paper and hands it to you. Any Chinese person knows that you need to take this "document" to the laboratory, called in Chinese the "huàyànshì" (hwah-yen-shure).

So you take your piece of paper and try to locate the lab, which may be on some other floor of the hospital entirely. You once again wade through a sea of people until you find the room that serves as the laboratory. You force your way in and give your precious slip of paper to another stern-faced woman, who looks like she went to the same charm school as the matron in the doctor's office. Now let's say they require a stool sample from you. The lab worker will immediately give you a small box made of paper in which you are to deposit your stool sample. For a urine sample you are given a little cup, much like in the States. The lab does not have its own designated facility for collecting samples, so you will need to find the nearest restroom. When you find the lavatory, you discover that it's inevitably a squat toilet. You get on your haunches and use the tiny paper-made box to squeeze your stool sample from your buttocks into the little container. It's a trick worthy of the finest contortionist and requires great precision. Often you're given a toothpick so you, and we're not kidding here, can skewer your stool sample from the toilet bowl, allowing you to pick it up and place it—like an hors d'oeuvre—in the box.

You put the lid on the little paper box and walk back to the lab. It's just one more humiliating moment after another as you walk past the crowd of waiting people with your stool sample in hand. Now it's time to wait again outside the lab for the results.

You will probably be called twenty or thirty minutes later and the results given to you on yet another piece of paper. You take the paper with the lab results back to your doctor.

Since you were gone the doctor has of course been seeing other patients, so once again you need to wait until the doctor will see you again. Now you become one of those onlookers whom you resented only moments before, listening in on other patients' problems. Eventually you are able to sit down again across from the doctor. He or she will inform you what illness you have and give you a prescription. Everything will be written down in the little booklet. The physician keeps no record at all of your diagnosis or your treatment. So hold onto that little booklet for your next visit to the hospital. Of course if you have some extensive test or operation, the hospital will keep a record of this, just as in a western hospital.

You then take your prescription back to the lobby. Before going to the pharmacy in the hospital you must go to the "Accounts Window" ("huàjiàchù" or hwah-gee-ah-choo). Here they will calculate the cost of the medicine and demand that you pay first.

Some hospitals then have you get in another line to pay, but if you're lucky the "Cashier's Window" and the "Accounts Window" are one and the same.

You must pay cash, unless you are a Chinese person with an insurance policy that covers you. Foreigners always have to pay cash at these ordinary Chinese hospitals.

After you pay, your piece of paper with your prescription will be stamped. You then go to yet another line to pick up your medicine. Very likely by this time of the day, there is a long line at the cashier's window as well as at the pharmacy window.

If you just require one or two common medications, the pharmacist will probably gather them right way and throw them at you under the window. If there are a number of prescriptions to be filled, however, and especially if Chinese herbal medicines are required, you will need to wait. This wait can be as "short" as thirty minutes or as long as an hour or two. By this time, even if you showed up at the hospital at 7:30 in the morning, it may very well now be close to 5:00 in the afternoon.

Let's say you also need an injection in addition to the prescription. After you pay the money at the cashier's window in the lobby, you then go the Inoculations Room with your receipt and get your shot. If you have a fever and they need to take your temperature, do not expect that they will simply stick a thermometer in your ear for a few seconds, as they now do in the States. No, it's the good old-fashioned mercury thermometer that we Baby Boomers knew back in our childhood.

There are reforms being enacted in the Chinese medical system in recent years, just as in every other aspect of Chinese life. But throughout the latter part of the twentieth century the above "day in the life of a Chinese out-patient" was common in all Chinese hospitals. You need to be prepared for this still, should you fall ill outside of one of the major cities in China. If you're unfortunate enough to go to a regular Chinese hospital as described above, prepare for that to be your activity for the entire day.

Be sure to check with your local health care professionals to find out what immunizations they might recommend for China. Although no shots are required for short-term stays, we particularly suggest you update your inoculations for hepatitis, which is a sufficient concern in the U.S. but which is extremely widespread in China.

Encountering the Unusual

Whenever you travel anywhere in the world you have to be ready to expect the unexpected. A train might be late, or your plane can't take off because of bad weather, or you end up losing your luggage. A tourist just has to be able to roll with the punches, knowing that very likely sooner or later something unforeseen might pop up. If that is true when traveling around America or France, it is even truer when visiting a developing nation like China.

Let us tell you a few stories of unexpected circumstances that Larry has been faced with in his travels around China with his students. Even though these events happened several decades back, when the country was nowhere as developed for tourism nor as economically advanced as it is now, here are a few examples of the weird kind of things that fate just might throw at you. Even in China of the twenty-first century, it's still possible to encounter the unusual.

Trouble on the Tracks

It's the summer of 1984. Larry was taking an overnight train with his college students from the city of Chengdu in

Sichuan Province to the mile-high city of Kunming in the southwestern province of Yunnan. Today most tourists would take a plane from one city to the other and arrive in an hour or two. But in the early 1980s you took a train.

Larry and his small band of followers had been riding the rails for eight hours or more when suddenly, around five o'clock in the morning, the train they were on came to an abrupt halt. Larry looked around and saw in the light of dawn that they had stopped in the middle of nowhere, and that nowhere was somewhere in the mountains of Sichuan Province. The only sign of civilization was a small village that lay down a steep hill from the railroad tracks.

Larry asked the conductor why the train had stopped in such an out-of-the-way spot. It was explained to him that there had been a rock slide which had blocked the tracks directly ahead. When Larry inquired as to when the track ahead might be cleared, the conductor replied that most likely it wouldn't be until around two or three o'clock in the afternoon. That was nine or ten hours later!

So Larry decided to make the best use of the time he could. He got up out of his "first-class" or "soft sleeper" compartment and proceeded to walk through the train to see if he could find some interesting people with whom to converse. He finally made his way to the "third class" section of the train, namely the "hard seat" cars at the back of the train. Here he discovered various young foreigners from a variety of countries, who were either traveling alone or

with a friend. These young Westerners included a young male college student from France, a young female doctor from Germany, and a young blonde couple from the Netherlands. All of them had been backpacking around China for some time, but none of them spoke any Chinese.

After getting to know these very nice young people, Larry had a brilliant notion.

Instead of just sitting on the train for the next nine or ten hours, reading a Harlequin romance or trying to sleep, why not venture out into the small village that lay below them? It certainly looked very idyllic in the early morning sun. A trip through the village would reveal what Chinese peasant life was all about. And Larry could act as translator for the young foreign travelers who had been dying to ask the Chinese all sorts of questions but were unable to do so because of the language barrier.

Larry went back to wake up his students and see which members of the group wanted to accompany him. Larry's sister and five of the students were anxious to join the small party of explorers, which included all the young Europeans. Larry asked the conductor whether it would be alright if they ventured out into the small village nearby. He was told that it was fine, but that he and his friends should return to the train no later than noon, since it was possible the track might be cleared by then. Larry neglected to inform his Chinese tour guide of his departure from the train, but figured that was unimportant since the conductor had given him permission to leave. Larry's friend, Norm, however, who had served in the Vietnam War and was always a bit wary of possible problems, decided to remain on the train along with the sleepier, less adventurous students.

When this small party of brave explorers walked down the hill from the railroad tracks toward the village below, they were excited. Here was a quite ancient village with cobblestone streets and red mud-brick houses amidst jade-green rice fields. Water buffalo were grazing leisurely in the rice paddies and ducks were wandering all over the village. As if they had taken some time machine, the group felt themselves transported back to a previous century. It was a small village as it turned out, with only around three thousand inhabitants. The people there welcomed them, especially because Larry and his students spoke Chinese. Incredibly, Larry's group was informed that the people of that village had not encountered any Westerners for nearly four decades!

After visiting the few shops to be found in the village, Larry and friends spotted a school in the distance and made

their way toward it. As with all schools in China, there was a high wall that completely enclosed the school grounds. Larry's impromptu tour group entered the school via the main gate, unannounced and uninvited. They looked a bit like a college students' mock delegation from the United Nations, since they represented at least four different countries. The hair color of the group pretty much covered the entire spectrum from blonde and bright red through most shades of brown and black.

The heads of Chinese children of all ages popped out of all the windows of the classrooms on seeing this group of strangers appear in the courtyard of their school. After all, this was a village that hadn't seen a "white" visitor in nearly 40 years. Now suddenly there was a whole group of them!

In another instant the entire school of seven hundred students, together with their teachers, was out in the courtyard, surrounding the little foreign band of travelers. All the scheduled activities of the school had come to a screeching halt in order to face this invasion of aliens who had seemingly dropped in upon them out of the sky.

The group of foreigners was greeted very warmly, indeed, as all the Chinese children crowded round them for a closer look. Some of the children wanted to touch the white skin and blonde hair of the Dutch couple. Others were fascinated by the fur on Larry's hairy arms and couldn't resist feeling it.

Larry explained to the Chinese teachers that they were foreign tourists who were interested in seeing what a Chinese school was like. The principal of the school let them sit in on an English class, during which students dutifully repeated after their teacher meaningful phrases like "What is this? It is a chair. What is this? It is a cat."

But first the students insisted on challenging the foreigners to several games of ping-pong on tables that had bricks in the middle in place of nets. Larry and his group one by one all were defeated soundly by the little Chinese grade school children they faced on the other side of the little brick wall. But they had broken down that bigger wall that too often separates people from different cultures. They had made friends with the Chinese children.

When Larry's group left the school several hours later, they were seen off by the entire school. All the children and teachers waved and smiled, as the foreigners retreated back down the cobblestone walkway toward the village. The young Europeans as well as Larry and his students were elated by this unexpected chance to see a Chinese rural school up close. They had enjoyed an extraordinary experience that they would never forget.

Everything would have been fine had the group returned to the train at this point.

But greedy for still more adventures of this kind, Larry spotted a wide river at the back of the village, beyond which lay some peasant homes and rice fields on a steep hillside. Behind those homes and fields high mountains rose up majestically. Larry, who had appointed himself tour guide for the whole group, also spied a long, narrow wood-plank bridge that spanned the river. The group headed for the bridge, thinking that if they crossed it another amazing adventure would most likely be theirs.

When they approached the wood-plank bridge, however, they noticed that it was a very rickety old structure, with wooden slats to walk on that looked none too strong.

They also noticed that the river far below the bridge was moving very rapidly and that there was a good deal of whitewater where the river dashed over the rocks in its way.

Much as the group wanted to cross that bridge to see the picturesque mud-brick peasant homes and rice paddies on the other side, they hesitated to cross a bridge that seemed so flimsy. Just then a herd boy passed them leading a flock of 30-40 goats. The boy and his goats marched directly onto the bridge and soon had crossed over safely to the other side.

Seeing this and deciding it might be safe for them after all, one by one Larry and his foreign band of travelers walked very gingerly over the fifty-foot long bridge. On the other side was what seemed to them a mini Shangri-La on the lush green slopes of the mountain. A few peasants were working leisurely in the fields near the river. When they saw the foreign contingent approach, they immediately laid down their hoes and asked the group to come into their home. Soon a whole group of peasants appeared at their neighbor's doorway to view the aliens close up. One peasant cut some sugar cane from out in the nearby fields and presented a big stalk to each of the tourist group to chew on.

While sucking the sweet juice from the cane, Larry translated as the young Europeans took turns asking the peasants questions about their families, their way of life, and their views on everything from taxes to religion. Everyone seemed to be having a great time in this cultural exchange. A sense of timelessness came over the foreigners as they savored the chance to visit with Chinese peasants in what to the Westerners seemed a retreat from the hustle and bustle of the modern world.

Suddenly the young Frenchman turned to Larry and said: "Do you hear that? "

Larry was too engrossed in conversation with the Chinese to have heard anything else.

When he was quiet and listened, however, he did indeed

hear the sound that had caught the Frenchman's attention. It was the distant but distinct sound of a train whistle.

Larry looked at his watch. It was 1:30 in the afternoon! He had promised to be back before noon! Larry shouted: "It's every man for himself! I've got to get back to the train first, since I'm the only one who can speak Chinese fluently!"

Larry quickly thanked the peasants for their hospitality and dashed out of their home, with his coterie of followers at his heels. He ran down the green mountainside toward the river. Suddenly he realized with horror that he had led his group nearly a mile over hill and field from the railroad tracks. The rickety wooden plank bridge that he had crossed so gingerly when going away from the village he this time raced across as if being chased by demons. The bridge quivered from side to side from his weight, but he dashed on. Running through the rice paddies he saw the ducks and geese scatter before him. The water buffalo simply turned their heads lazily, wondering what all this commotion was about.

The sound of the train whistle was growing louder now as Larry neared the rise in the hill before him, above which stood the train. His breathing was coming in big gasps. He wanted to stop and catch his breath, but there was no time. The train was about to leave his group stranded in the remote mountains of Sichuan Province!

And it was then that he thought he heard the voice of God, across the plains, calling him home:

"Laaarrrryyy . . . ! Laaaarrryyy . . . !" came the cry, urging him on.

But the voice was that of his Chinese guide, "Little" Guan, who had borrowed a bullhorn from the conductor and who was desperately trying to retrieve these stray foreigners before the train took off. Thoughts of a long prison stint for losing a tourist group in the countryside must have been racing through his tortured mind.

Finally Larry managed to climb up the embankment onto the railroad tracks, right in front of where the train stood. Waving his arms like a madman, Larry shouted in Chinese: "Wait! Wait! The others are coming! The others are coming!" He turned around to see the group of a dozen or so young Westerners running in a twisted line through the rice paddies below.

When Larry entered the train it was through the door to a train car that held at least a hundred Chinese. It turned out that a nearby army group had cleared the track by 11:30 in the morning. The seven hundred Chinese passengers had been waiting there for two hours. Our Chinese guide had begged the conductor to blow the whistle to warn us to return, but was told that they couldn't blow the whistle unless

they started the train. And if they started the train they didn't have enough fuel to let it idle for long before taking off. Finally at 1:30 the whistle was blown.

Instead of hurling insults at the inconsiderate foreigner who had made them all wait an additional two hours, all the Chinese on the train were anxious to ask him questions. None of them had ever met a foreigner who spoke their language fluently before. They were anxious to inquire how he had learned Chinese, where he was from, and what he was doing in China. Larry just wanted to find a hole where he could hide his head in shame.

When the last of the stragglers had finally climbed aboard and the train got underway, Larry slunk back into his first-class compartment where his friend, Norm, was waiting for him. Norm gently chewed him out for being so irresponsible. "I knew there might be trouble as soon as you stepped off the train. That's why I thought I better stay here and keep watch over the other half of your students," his friend informed him.

It's unlikely that in today's China you will encounter an avalanche that will stop your train. Transportation is much more highly developed in present-day China and, as we said earlier, these days most foreign tourists would have managed this journey in less than two hours by air instead of a long overnight railway trip. Nevertheless there are several important lessons to learn from Larry's experience:

When given the chance to see China off the beaten track, definitely take it. You'll see the country in a way few foreigners are able.

Do, however, always be considerate of your Chinese hosts. You are a guest in their country and they are responsible for you. If you promise you will return to an appointed place at an appointed hour, make sure you keep your promise! Return a bit early rather than late! If you make hundreds of Chinese wait for you for two hours just because you can't tell time, they might not be as understanding as Larry's fellow passengers.

Bus Boondoggle

This story comes from the same ill-fated trip as the adventure above.

Larry had decided that his group must see one of the sacred mountains of China known as Mt. Emei. He had read of its legendary beauty, of the lush green hillsides, of the wild monkeys that lived on its slopes, and of the peak where one could walk above the clouds. The original plan was to do what most Chinese visitors to the mountain had done for centuries, namely hike the twenty or so miles up the winding mountain trail the first day, stay at the old Buddhist temple at the summit overnight, and walk back down the following day. His Chinese guide, the aforementioned "Little" Guan, had advised that the group save its strength (as well as his new black leather shoes) and ride the bus the first day to the end of the line around three miles from the top. From there they could then walk up the rest of the way. He also persuaded the tired group of travelers that the second day they could retrace their steps to the bus stop and ride most of the way down as well.

All went well the first day. The bus snaked up the winding mountain road until there was no longer a road to follow. The group got off at the small bus station there and walked alongside hundreds of Chinese travelers until they reached the top.

The view was magnificent, if a bit obscured by the mountain mists that cover the mountain for most of the year.

At night Larry's group saw a small group of Chinese college students gathered around a fire not too far from the ancient temple which at that time was the only place to stay at the summit. The Chinese were from many different provinces and were entertaining each other in true Chinese fashion. They were taking turns singing folksongs or doing folk dances from their respective provinces. Larry's group had to finally reciprocate by singing a few American folksongs. As the Americans launched into a spirited rendition of "I've Been Working on the Railroad," Larry realized something was terribly wrong. His friend, Norm, was singing with gusto, but he was completely tone deaf! Singing was obviously not going to endear them to their new Chinese friends, Larry thought. They were there to create friendships across cultures, not start a war! So Larry immediately launched into a comedy routine, telling jokes about a foreigner in China who kept butchering the Chinese language. The hearty laughter of the Chinese students made him think briefly of resigning his teaching job in America and becoming a stand-up comic in China.

After sleeping soundly among the ghosts in the old temple, Larry and his group awoke the next morning to a tremendous downpour of rain. Having prepared for this eventuality, the group put on their flimsy rain ponchos and started the soggy walk down the ancient stone steps to the bus station three miles down the road.

When they reached the shelter of the station, however, they discovered that the small building was packed to the rafters with soaked Chinese travelers who had been waiting for several hours for the bus to come. Suddenly bad news made its way quickly through the crowd. The heavy rain had washed out the road up the mountain. Mudslides had blocked the road and it was impossible for the bus to make it up the mountain that morning and possibly for the rest of the day.

It was then that Larry made his fateful decision. Since there was no guarantee that the bus would come that day and since there was no room for them to wait in the shelter anyway, they would walk the whole way down . . . in the rain! Seventeen miles, in fact.

The group started out together. It was rough going, since the path had been laid out centuries ago with huge stone steps that were only comfortable to walk down if you had the stride of a giant. And the steps were very slippery in the rain. It was soon obvious that the more athletic members of the group could descend two or three times faster than the slowest member of the group, one of whom was Larry's sister, Nancy. The main reason his sister was so slow was that she had insisted on wearing the traditional black cotton shoes commonly worn by most people in China. However, these were shoes definitely not designed for mountain climbing!

It wasn't until nearly nightfall that Larry managed to escort his sister all the way down to the foot of the mountain and the safety of the bus. They had walked in the rain for nearly twelve hours and were soaked to the bone. Right at dusk, however, the rain had finally stopped and the sun made a guest appearance to deliver a lovely sunset. As a weary brother and sister trudged along the path through the village at the foot of the mountain, sympathetic peasants sitting by their doorsteps invited the two in for a meal and some rest. Grateful as they were, the two tired travelers surmised that Larry's students had all long ago reached the bus and were waiting for them. Thanking the villagers for their kind offer but unable to accept, Larry and his sister fi-

nally climbed aboard the bus. It was by now pitch black outside. They could at least return to their guesthouse and not have to spend the night on the rain-soaked slopes of Mt. Emei.

Even the most athletic members of Larry's group had sore knees from walking down a mountain for twenty miles. All of them had been amused when they had been presented with walking canes at the beginning of their visit to the mountain, canes engraved with the characters "I climbed Mt. Emei." Why would young, hearty college students like them ever need walking sticks to climb a mountain? But for the next three days everyone in the group came to rely on those canes to even negotiate the steps in and out of the tour bus. When they came to steps in the lobby of the hotel where next they stayed, the group would cry out in unison, "Oh, no! Steps!" Since these were all young college students, the Chinese in the hotel must have gotten the notion that Americans were so out of shape that even their young people needed canes to walk with. And they were so spoiled and in such poor physical condition that to merely negotiate a few stairs was a big undertaking for them!

Always check the weather forecast before embarking on

a mountain climbing adventure like this. In the early 1980s, when Larry led his group to Mt. Emei, there was no Internet to consult. Now, thanks to websites like weather.com, you can at least get some idea of whether or not a torrential downpour or monsoon rain is expected.

Unless you're traveling to the Sahara or Gobi Deserts, always bring some rain gear, preferably a good-quality rain poncho. An umbrella is nice for city touring, but is of little use when climbing twenty miles down a mountain in a driving rain.

If you don't think you can walk downhill in the rain for twenty miles, just wait for the bus. We heard that on the fateful day described above, the bus did finally arrive at the bus station near the top of the mountain by the middle of the afternoon. "They are served, too, who only stand and wait," as the poet Milton might have observed had he been there.

Stinky Armpits and other Hygiene Tales

Since China's swift modernization in the past few decades, most of the products that we Westerners rely upon in our daily lives are now available in the Middle Kingdom.

If you forgot to pack your razor blades or hair spray or aspirin, you won't have much trouble finding a store in China where you can buy them. The four and five-star hotels in China where the majority of us Westerners stay provide you with complimentary shampoo, toothpaste, and combs anyway. But there are a few things that you still better make sure you bring along from your home country, because you'll have a devil of the a time finding them in China. The most critical example that springs to mind is deodorant.

Deodorant is an extremely commonplace item in countries like the U.S., where few people dare go out in public without anointing themselves under both armpits with the stuff in one form or another. Because a person's own natural body odor is generally not appreciated by his (and, sometimes, her) fellow human beings, deodorant helps keep our society on a civil footing by making it bearable to be with our neighbor at close quarters. In China, however, almost no one uses deodorant and it's nearly impossible to find it in any store other than large stores like Wal-Mart and Carrefour.

Chinese pharmacies, unlike their Western counterparts, do not carry products like shampoo or deodorant, but only medicine. Supermarkets in America always have a section for things like deodorant.

When Larry was coming perilously close to running out of deodorant on our last trip around China, we entered a

fancy department store in a large Chinese city. We were con-
fident that if they didn't have such a product, they would at
least be able to direct us to some store that could save Qin's
delicate sensibilities and hence save our marriage.

Even though Qin grew up in China and although we are
both long-time professors of Chinese, we did not even know
what the Chinese might call this invaluable elixir for preserv-
ing social harmony. The old phrase that Larry had learned
in Taiwan three decades ago, namely "water for eliminating
body odor," certainly didn't register with store clerks in today's mainland China. We explained that we wanted to buy
some kind of cologne ("fragrant water" in Chinese) that you
put under your arms to smell better. Most clerks would tell
us simply that they had a vague notion of what we meant,
but that their store definitely carried no such product. Finally one clerk told us that what we wanted was "tǐ xiāng
shuǐ" (tee-sheeang-shway or "body fragrant water") and
that we could buy it at a British pharmacy across the street.
Sure enough, when entering that pharmacy we breathed a
sigh of relief as we spied the name Gillette on many of their
products, including deodorant.

The point of all this is that, despite how modern cities
like Beijing and Shanghai have become, you can often get
lulled into a false sense of security (remember the section
on bathrooms at the beginning of the book?). Don't take
anything for granted, and do not always count on finding
everything you might need. In places that are more off the

beaten track, which are increasingly popular with Western tourists, shopping for what you might have left behind at home becomes all the more difficult. So besides making absolutely sure you have packed your own prescription medicines that you rely on, be sure to pack ordinary things like deodorant as well.

The following is a story that happened to that same star-crossed student group that Larry led on an adventurer's tour of China in the 1980s. It will help us emphasize that when you travel the globe, always make sure to carry with you the most essential items. You cannot depend on being able to pick them up just anywhere. This includes feminine hygiene products.

Back in the early 1980s one of the best places to go to see China off the beaten path was the jungle area in southeastern Yunnan Province known as Xishuangbanna (See-shwahng-bah-nah). With a name that sounds a bit like "she swang banana," this lush area of banana trees and elephants lies near China's border with Laos and Burma. Somewhat sadly, this region is now completely developed for tourism, but back in the '80s few foreign tour groups ever visited this remote part of the country. Instead of the myriad hotels that now accommodate visitors, there was only one guesthouse acceptable to foreigners.

Larry thought it would be exciting to see what was then an unspoiled part of China, where the Dai minority people wore colorful costumes, lived in houses built on stilts, and

farmed with water buffalo. In those days the fastest way to reach this area was to take a small twin-prop plane to the nearest city with an airport, then take a bus ride of around seven hours over hilly terrain to reach the small town from which the group planned to explore the surrounding jungle for the next three days.

Perhaps it was the Chinese tour guide's fault for not explaining more clearly to Larry about how the baggage for this trip was to be handled. Or perhaps Larry had not listened carefully enough to the guide's explanation when the two were drinking beer together the night before they embarked on this adventure. Whoever was to blame, Larry and his students did not realize that when the guide asked the American group to leave their suitcases outside their doors the next morning before departing their hotel in the provincial city of Kunming, they would not be seeing their luggage again for three days. Wasn't it obvious that neither the tiny twin-prop plane nor the mini-bus they would take to get to the jungle could possibly hold the large suitcases with which Westerners travel? Unfortunately this was not at all obvious to Larry and his students.

Larry's group did not suspect anything was wrong until they had survived a bumpy plane ride on a plane that would have looked familiar to Baron von Richthofen, and found themselves on an even bumpier bus headed for the jungle area. One of Larry's female students suddenly turned to her teacher, whom she had always trusted, and asked: "Where is our luggage?" She had astutely noticed, you see, that the group's suitcases were not in the bus with them. "Oh, they're probably coming along behind us in another bus," Larry replied without total confidence. "No, they're not," piped up the Chinese guide. "They'll be waiting for you at the hotel in Kunming when we go back there three days from now." Larry's group suddenly turned surly. He realized how Captain Bligh must have felt when most of his crew on the *Bounty* turned against him.

After all, almost no one had anything with them except the clothes on their backs, their money, and their passports. The only one who had a clean change of underwear or even a toothbrush was Larry's friend, Norm. Norm had been all around the world and always made sure he had the bare essentials on his person at all times in a small tote bag.

Now it was the women in Larry's group who turned the most hostile. This was not due to the fact, as some of you men might hastily conclude, that in a crisis women are more excitable than men. No, it was because of an incredible coincidence: all of the women except Larry's sister, Nancy, were experiencing that once-a-month discomfort known euphemistically as a "period." It was one thing to be without a change of underwear or a toothbrush for three days. Underwear and other clothes could be washed out in the sink each night. You can at least rinse your mouth and use your fingers to clean your teeth. But to be without basic feminine hygiene items for three whole days was flat out asking too much of the women in Larry's long-suffering tour group. Remember that this was the same bunch of people who had needed to run for their lives to keep from being left behind in a village in the mountains of Sichuan Province. And this was the same group of people who had walked twenty miles down Mt. Emei in the rain.

"Don't panic, people," croaked the Captain Bligh of college tour groups. "Surely there will be a store on the way where you can buy what you need," Larry said to comfort the upset ladies.

"There isn't any town where we're headed, only a small village," cautioned the Chinese guide. For the next five hours or so it was very quiet on the bus as the women sulked and Larry vowed to lock his door securely that night to keep from being lynched. Finally the bus came within sight of a small group of stalls set up alongside the road, where they sold a variety of merchandise. Larry asked the driver to stop there so that they could attempt to buy something—anything that would help the women. Accompanied by his oldest female student, Larry went up to the minority women who were in charge of these roadside stalls.

There they dis-
covered toothbrush-
es, toothpaste, soap,
towels—all the
things they most
craved at this point.
Was it too much
to hope they would also

have feminine napkins? When Larry explained to these minority women that the ladies in his group were having their
period, the Dai women immediately grasped the situation.
They took out a large amount of what looked to Larry like
pink crepe paper and handed it to him.

Larry's female student was totally at a loss as to how to
use this crepe paper to solve her problem. The Dai women
explained that women in China knew how to use string to
keep the paper in its intended place. Larry asked that they be
so kind as to pantomime to his student how to do this, while
he beat a hasty retreat to the bus. The Dai women willingly
obliged. Larry and his other students watched from the bus
as the minority women showed Larry's student how to create a maxi-pad: Chinese style. When the woman student returned to the bus and they drove away, waving a thank-you
to the Dai women, the Americans could not help but notice
that the minority women were not just smiling but were con-
vulsed with laughter at the seeming insanity of it all: these

strange foreigners who had dropped in out of nowhere, asking for a lesson in how to use feminine napkins!

Equipped with enough crepe paper to decorate a hundred bicycles for a Fourth of July parade, the women in Larry's group were able to make it through the next three days. His students' dignity and clothing (not to mention Larry's life) were all saved.

Mass Protests
and General Mayhem

When visiting China it is highly unlikely you will encounter any kind of civil war, such as tourists fear in parts of Africa. You most probably will also not have to worry about any armed insurrection or violent protest against the government. Unlike countries where people celebrate weddings by shooting AK-47s in the air, citizens in China are not allowed to own guns, nor, frankly, are they really interested in doing so. China as yet has also not been the scene of any terrorist attacks, although there is always concern about Muslim uprisings in the province of Xinjiang in the far west of the country. There is also no "mafia" (as we know it) operating in China. Violent crime such as armed robbery or murder is far less common in China than in the U.S. One benefit of an authoritarian state like China is that this is a government that knows how to maintain the rule of law and public order. There is simply no other practical way to run a country of 1.3 billion people, even if in Western eyes that means greatly curtailing individual civil liberties and human rights. China is among the safer countries in the world to visit. The stability of the Chinese government is a big factor in making foreign companies feel less risk involved with doing business there.

However, in any country that is not a democracy there is always a chance you might encounter some kind of mass demonstration or even violent clashes with government troops. When Larry took students to China in the late spring of 1989, they did encounter mass protests and a government crackdown that drew the attention of the entire world.

Throughout the 1980s life in China became gradually freer and more prosperous after the horrible repression of the Cultural Revolution that squelched all freedoms in the decade from 1966 to 1976. Once purged by Mao, Deng Xiaoping had emerged from six years of prison and isolation to eventually lead China on a series of major economic reforms. Deng established the Special Economic Zones in southern China, which were a test bed for international and joint venture projects that served to put China on the world stage as a leader in manufacturing. In an atmosphere of rising expectations, by the spring of 1989, mass protests led by college students sprang up in several big cities in China, including Beijing. The students had been spurred to action over the death of Hu Yaobang, a reform-minded leading cadre who had been stripped of power. They saw Hu's treatment as representative of everything that was wrong with the party. The world was watching China, eagerly anticipating the arrival of Soviet leader Mikhail Gorbachev in Beijing, which herald-

ed the official return of Sino-Soviet ties. But the Gorbachev story was lost amid a sea of students and other "protest-ers" who gathered in front of the Great Hall of the People in Tiananmen Square. These idealistic young people demanded an end to government corruption, called for a free press, and clamored for greater social and politi-cal freedom. As media cameras from all over the globe were trained on the square, there was the hope that China might even become a democracy.

When Larry took off for China with his students near the end of May, 1989, they were excited at the prospect of seeing the protests in Tiananmen Square up close. They wanted to cheer on the students and perhaps even speak with some of them. Their itinerary included three days in Beijing at the beginning of June.

The first week of their travels in the south of the coun-try was peaceful, as the group enjoyed the skyscrapers of Hong Kong and the beautiful lush mountain scenery of Gui-lin. When they reached the southwestern city of Chengdu, however, it was a different landscape entirely. The streets everywhere in the downtown area were crowded with peo-ple who were part of a mass protest led by students and

workers gathered in the city square.

The Americans' tour bus had trouble entering the compound of the hotel where they were staying because of the huge crowds of people blocking the way. Their hotel, the main place for foreigners to stay, was four blocks from the city square at the center of town, yet the streets were jammed with people all the way from the square to past the entrance of their hotel on the main street.

The next day, June 4, Larry led his students through the crowds to try to speak with some of the protesters. What was later estimated to be around a quarter of a million Chinese people from all walks of life were out on the streets of Chengdu to show support for this freedom movement. Many were willing to talk to Larry's group about their hope for change and for some bigger freedoms in the future. Impressed by their earnestness and expressing their support, Larry started to lead his small band of students back to their hotel. When they reached the outer limit of the crowd, suddenly a rumor spread that government troops were coming. Everyone started running away from the square and it seemed to Larry that it was a good time to beat it back to the hotel. When his students saw their teacher run, he who had before then shown no fear, they took to their heels as well, most of them passing him on their way to the safety of the hotel lobby.

That night Larry and his group watched from the rooftop restaurant of their hotel as they saw the crowds gather again in the square. Government troops had indeed marched into the city. The Americans, along with a handful of other foreign tourists, watched with horror as they saw the Chinese soldiers start to clear the square by force. It was much like the cruel end to the Tiananmen protests, but this was happening in Chengdu, the provincial capital of Sichuan, without any foreign TV reporters or cameramen present.

From their rooftop perch Larry and his students could see the unarmed populace try to barricade themselves behind buses that they overturned and set ablaze. The army lobbed tear gas at them and started using their bayonets to drive out the angry yet fearful crowds. Ambulances with red crosses passed the hotel, trying to make it to the wounded in the middle of the action. When Larry's intrepid students heard gunfire in the air, they rushed to their rooms and hid under their beds. This surely wasn't real but just a movie being staged, Larry remembered feeling at the time.

The next morning when Larry and his students made their way gingerly down to the first floor of the hotel for breakfast, they saw broken glass all over the lobby. The giant blue and white vases, as tall as a man, had been smashed. There were traces of blood here and there in the washrooms and on the lobby floor. It seemed protesters had sought refuge in their hotel lobby and been forced out by the soldiers.

A haze of tear gas hung heavy in the air as Larry and his students walked the now deserted streets of downtown Chengdu. They saw burned-out buses and trolley cars in the center of one of China's most modern and prosperous cities. The people of the city, who had been so friendly and anxious to talk to the Americans several days before, were now too afraid and too much in shock to even greet them. There was little point in staying in Chengdu any longer after such a horror had devastated the city. So Larry did the only logical thing. He took a flight with his students directly to Beijing; they arrived a day after the Tiananmen Massacre.

When Larry's group rode the bus from the airport to their hotel, they passed Tiananmen Square. The world's largest public square that lies in front of the Forbidden City was filled with soldiers and tanks and tents. The army was bivouacked there to keep the peace after they had cleared out by force the thousands of protesters gathered there just the day before.

After checking into their hotel in Beijing, Larry received a phone call from the American Embassy. He was told that all foreigners including Americans were advised to not go out of their hotel for any reason, in case there should be more violence. The American Embassy also informed him that all

Americans should leave China as soon as they could find a flight out. Larry and his students found themselves virtual prisoners in the hotel, holed up there with foreign tourists and businesspeople from various other Western countries. They were slightly scared, but mostly they were bored.

With every foreigner attempting to leave China all at the same time, Larry's group had to remain in Beijing for the next few days. His local Chinese guide in Beijing suggested that, since Larry had paid in advance for his group to be taken out to the Great Wall, perhaps they should make use of this time and go see China's most famous tourist site. It was a surreal scene, as almost no Chinese were on the streets of Beijing when Larry's bus pulled out of the hotel and headed out of town toward the Great Wall.

After several hours of travel, as the bus began to climb a steep hill within a mile of the Great Wall, it suddenly came to a halt. The bus had broken down and needed to be repaired. Since they were so close to the Wall and didn't know how long the repairs would take, the young group of Americans decided to walk the rest of the way.

As they began the steep climb up the hill, they could not help but notice that there were no people around anywhere. In fact, in this crowded land they had barely seen anyone out on the roads for many miles. They could hear what they thought were cannons or big guns going off in the distance. It was Spring, but Larry was feeling the heat of summer. He was also in a phase of life where he did "heavy

hands" weight training whenever he could, to stay in shape. Taking off his shirt and seizing his small dumbbells, a bare-chested Larry went along swinging his arms back and forth as he and the Chinese guide led the students up the hill toward the Great Wall.

Suddenly they noticed that coming down the hill right toward them was a long procession of army tanks and jeeps. Chinese soldiers rode on top of each, with machine guns at the ready. Larry and his students found themselves face to face with at least several hundred Chinese troops armed to the teeth. This was not exactly the kind of encounter with Chinese people that Larry had planned for his students on the trip!

As the soldiers rode by stone-faced, the Chinese guide cursed them under his breath. Larry, however, advised his students to just smile and walk on. Fortunately the soldiers were not interested in a small group of young Americans that were too stupid to know they should remain inside their hotel, and rode by without incident.

Larry's group did have an extremely rare opportunity to walk along the Great Wall without any other tourists in sight. Usually the wall is packed with visitors from all over the world. That day, however, the American tour group had the Wall all to themselves. Larry was still intent on doing his "heavy hands." Leaving his T-shirt in a crevice on the Wall, he led his students a good mile or more along this marvel of ancient engineering. When he came back to pick up his shirt, it was gone! No one around for miles, at least as far as they could see, and yet his shirt had still been ripped off! Or had a bird—or perhaps the spirit of some long-dead Great Wall laborer—come and taken it away?

10

The People

We've spent a good part of this book complaining about the seemingly rude behavior of the Chinese people. Even though we understand some of the reasons why the Chinese act the way they do, namely that they live everyday in an overcrowded society where the average educational level is still very low, that doesn't make it any less aggravating when they cut in line or fail in the social niceties. And yet when our American friends return from a stay in China, whether it's a two-week trip or a long sojourn there, they invariably say that what they enjoyed most about the entire experience was "the people." They really like the Chinese people whom they had a chance to get to know. "The historical sites, the scenery, the food, everything was great. But most of all we really liked the Chinese people. They were so friendly, good-humored, and welcoming." This very positive reaction of our friends doesn't seem to jibe at all with the quite negative impression we've given so far of the Chinese in certain social situations. What, then, accounts for this seeming disparity?

The reason is that there are probably few societies in

the world that act in such a Jekyll-and-Hyde manner as the Chinese. When we ask our educated Chinese friends why their fellow Chinese are so rude in public situations, they all agree that in China there are two standards of conduct or morality in your relationships with other people. There is one code of conduct that the Chinese use in dealing with people they know and a completely different one for dealing with strangers—not foreigners, per se, but rather within the constantly turning wheels of society as a whole.

There are not many cultures in the world where people look out for their family members the way the Chinese do. In every country in the world parents make great sacrifices to give their children a better life. Not only is this very true in China, but more than in most societies the children in turn reciprocate later in life by making terrific sacrifices for their parents. After all, this is the country of "filial piety," where children are expected to go to any lengths to serve their parents in return for the gift of life which they enjoy. In the modern world the Chinese and the other peoples of East Asia assume a much bigger role in taking care of their aged parents than do people in the West, for whom retirement homes are the most common solution.

In addition, arguably no other culture in the world puts such a premium on friendship as do the Chinese. Friendship was one of the five sacred Confucian relationships, which have been stressed by Chinese society over the past 2,500 years.

Chinese will do almost anything for their friends, sometimes at great financial and personal sacrifice to themselves.

When it seemed that Qin's mother, who lives in Beijing, might need an extremely costly heart bypass procedure, the doctors insisted on having the Chinese equivalent of US$10,000 in cash before they would operate. We could not send a check for that amount because it would take a month for the check to be approved and cashed. We turned to our Chinese friends in Beijing for help, asking them to loan us the money. Given the fact that the average Chinese income is ⅟₃₀ that of the average American, US$10,000 was an astronomical amount of money for them to put together in just a few days. It would literally be like asking your American friends to loan you almost one hundred thousand dollars for an operation for your mother, with you promising to pay them back in a month. Four of Qin's friends pooled their resources and donated all their savings to loan us this money to try to save the life of Qin's mother. Fortunately for everyone (Qin's mother especially), the surgery was not needed after all, and the money was returned. But Qin's friends did not hesitate in offering immediate assistance, even if it meant spending every penny they had.

In China there is a very high standard of conduct, indeed, when it comes to taking care of friends and family. The same care and concern the Chinese show toward friends and family are also evident in their dealings with the foreign tourists and business associates whom they host. When you come to China as a member of a tourist group or business delegation, your Chinese hosts or guides will treat you as an honored guest.

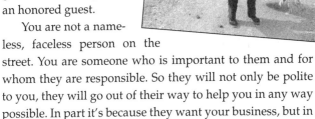

You are not a nameless, faceless person on the street. You are someone who is important to them and for whom they are responsible. So they will not only be polite to you, they will go out of their way to help you in any way possible. In part it's because they want your business, but in part it's because this is traditional Chinese hospitality.

When you venture out on the street on your own, however, you become a faceless and nameless person. Even as a foreigner, you are just another obstacle for the Chinese, who must deal all day long with the constant press and push of people in their effort to get where they need to go and do what they need to do. If you take even a few minutes to chat with the average Chinese person and get to know him or her just a little, most of the time you will find that they will then be very friendly and likeable indeed. If you make the effort to truly make friends with a Chinese person over a long period of time, you will never know a truer friend.

In the next chapter we deal with Chinese etiquette. Based on the early chapters in the book, we probably gave you the impression that the Chinese know nothing about etiquette or manners whatsoever. But there are many unspoken cultural rules about proper behavior when it comes to dealing with people whom you know. The Chinese will generally obey these unwritten rules of conduct we outline below when dealing with you, the foreign tourist or business person, just as they would with their friends and family members. You must recognize these rules and follow them in turn when dealing with the Chinese with whom you have meaningful contact. Leave the rules of the jungle that we have outlined in previous chapters for the jungle out on the streets. Let's now consider the Chinese at their civilized best.

A Basic Guide to Chinese Etiquette

Generally, the Chinese are quite informal people, much like Americans. Imagine a scale of one to ten to measure the spectrum of a culture's etiquette, with ten being at the extreme of, say, British aristocracy of the Victorian era, and one being John Belushi as Bluto in "Animal House." In general, Japan would probably rate a 10, England an 8, China a 3 and America, believe it or not, probably around a 6 or so. In discussing Chinese etiquette, we're not talking about the total lack of manners displayed by Chinese people on the street to people they don't know. We're talking about the etiquette in the Chinese business world as well as in the world of Chinese friendships. The Chinese system of etiquette is very subtle and often the visual clues are very hard to spot.

Below is a long list of "dos" and "don'ts." These are the basic rules for how to behave properly when doing business or interacting with your Chinese friends.

Meeting and Greeting People

Use a person's full name, never just their given name, when

you meet them for the first time. In China as in most East Asian countries, a person's surname, or family name, is usually said first, followed by the given name. This naming convention can sometimes be confusing. In the West, for example, we have become accustomed to seeing many Japanese names run in the familiar "Westernized" first-name, last-name convention, such as Akira Kurosawa, or Toshiro Mifune, when in fact in Japan it would be Kurosawa Akira or Mifune Toshiro. A lot of Westerners still don't realize that Chinese basketball superstar Yao Ming's surname is Yao. The vast majority of Chinese still use three characters in their name: The surname is one character and the given name is two characters. There are still rare two-character surnames, such as Ouyang (Ohyang) and Szto (Sigh-toe), but these are usually found in the south of China. Someone will hand you their business card and you will see three Chinese characters. Underneath (or on the back of the card) is usually written in English letters the person's name using the Chinese pinyin form of Romanization. For example, a man who is called Li Guoming is Mr. Li. When Romanized, the given name is usually written together as a single word, which is an immediate clue that Li, is, in fact the surname of the above gentleman. The more Chinese people you meet, the more you will get a feel for the many varieties of surnames out there. After a while, you will not only be able to figure out what a person's surname is based on the characters in their name, but, in some cases, also whether the person is a man or a woman. To confuse things a bit, however, these days some Chinese who are aware of our customs when meeting foreigners will give their name in the Western fashion, with their given name first. In these instances it is best to ask them for clarification as to which is their surname.

After you get to know Chinese people a little better, say after the second or third time you meet, you should no longer use their full names to address them. If you continue to do so as you develop a relationship, they will find it a bit stiff and off-putting. Adopt instead the Chinese custom of putting the word Lǎo (Old) in front of their surname if they are even a day older than you, or putting Xiǎo (Little) in front of their surname if they are even a day younger than you. This is a term of endearment that is a perfectly acceptable form of address. For example, if a Chinese friend's last name is Lǐ and he or she is older than you, begin to call him or her "Lǎo Lǐ" as you continue to meet. It does not matter if "Lǎo Lǐ" is only twenty-five years old. As long as he or she is older than you, it is perfectly appropriate, since it's just the Chinese way of showing affection in a relationship. And if a friend has the last name Chén and is younger than you, then you should start to address him or her as "Xiǎo Chén" as your friendship develops.

In a more formal setting such as in the business world, you'll want to address Chinese people as Mr. or Ms. from the first time you meet them, just as we would in Western countries. These days in the bigger cities shaking hands is an acceptable and common practice when people greet one another. Be warned: don't always expect to receive (or give) the "hey-how-are-ya-good-ta-see-ya" good ol' boy handshake that we Americans are so familiar with. Often times handshakes are photo opportunities: looks are sometimes better than substance. If you are meeting a woman, however, note that it is not as commonplace to shake hands. Wait until she extends her hand first. If the Chinese person does not extend his or her hand, don't miss a beat and don't interpret it as rudeness. Just simply nod or bow slightly from the shoulders. It is polite to make a slight gesture to yield the right of way to the Chinese you're getting to know at doorways, getting in cars, etc. If you are invited to visit, say, a school, factory, or some other place, the students or workers often will applaud you to both welcome you and to say goodbye. The appropriate way to respond is to applaud back with a smile. Chinese performers on the stage traditionally respond to the applause of their audience by applauding back. We've always found this a lovely custom that bespeaks humility and mutual respect. We're waiting for the day when the students at our college applaud us after a particularly inspired lesson, so we can applaud back.

Business Cards

If you are planning on doing business in China, it is essential that you bring a large supply of business cards with you. If you're only there as a tourist or a student, it is still a useful tool in making friends with the Chinese. Most Chinese in almost any walk of life have a business card. This is partially because there are so many homonyms in Chinese that a Chinese person cannot be certain how a person's name is written simply by hearing it. Only by seeing the pictographs for the person's name can they be certain how that name is written. Business cards also show a person's occupation and status in society, which is helpful in knowing with whom you are dealing. Finally the business card provides all sorts of practical information for contacting the other person. For Chinese people the business card or "míng-piàn" (ming-pee-en) is their identity. You are no one without it.

It is preferable if your business card has English on one side and Chinese on the other. This has become the norm for Chinese people in recent years, because of the rapidly growing contact with foreigners.

Present your card after the initial introductions, handshake, and courtesy bow.

Use both hands to present and receive cards. The Chinese and all East Asians generally use both hands to give or receive anything, especially in a formal setting. To give something with one hand is considered literally "offhanded," indifferent, and rude.

Remember that business cards in East Asia are an extension of the person. Therefore treat them with the utmost respect. This is a person's "face."

Do not write on business cards or play with them. Certainly do not put them in your back pocket and then sit down. You certainly don't want to sit on their "face"! After looking at the card carefully to note the person's name and position, it is best to hold it or place it in front of you. When you do put it away, place it in your wallet or front pocket, preferably in a cardholder just for that purpose.

Eating

When doing business in China, if the Chinese company with whom you're dealing is really interested in you they will certainly invite you to a big feast together. The Chinese do not believe in transacting any serious business before they've had at least a few good meals with any prospective business partners. If it's just a question of going out to eat with Chinese friends, however, it is necessary for you to realize that the Chinese do not believe in "Dutch treat."

They believe in "Chinese treat." This means that who-ever does the inviting in a circle of friends will be the one to order for the entire group and to pay the bill for everyone. Everyone understands that the next time someone else in the group will play the host and in turn pay for everyone.

When having a meal in a restaurant or anywhere else in China, you do not order or receive your own individual dish or dishes. The host orders a variety of different dishes for everyone to share. The waiter merely gives out one menu, which the host alone looks at. It is only he or she who will order. Careful not to grab the menu from the waiter's hands, or you'll end up paying for the meal! It is usually the custom to have a Lazy Susan or, as we like to call it, the "Wheel of Fortune." To help yourself to the common dishes that are beyond your reach at the table, simply spin the "Wheel of Fortune" slowly to have it stop with the desired dish before you. Do this carefully, of course, making sure that your Chi-nese friends are not right in the middle of ladling out the last of the birds nest soup! The group-oriented nature of East Asian society, as opposed to our Western individualism, is apparent in this communal way of eating.

Sample everything at the table to be polite, even if it's only a few bites. Do not be surprised if your Chinese host se-lects a few pieces of meat or seafood from the common dish-es with his own chopsticks and places them in your bowl with his chopsticks. This seems a bit domineering as well as unhygienic to a Westerner, but it is the Chinese host's way

 of showing that he wants to make sure his honored guest gets to sample the choicest morsels. Refusing any food is impolite, especially when offered like this . . . even if it's fried scorpion or roast cat. If you're at a formal banquet, which every Chinese organization will find any excuse to host, pace yourself. There are often a dozen or more courses!

Try to eat with chopsticks. They very likely may be the only eating utensils available anyway. Unless, that is, you carried a fork with you in your breast pocket all the way from your home country. If your Chinese business associate or friend is playing host, be sure to make some positive comments on the food. To not do so is considered rude.

Slurping noodles or soup or even your tea is acceptable. Burping is not considered rude, either. Also be aware that making the sound "mmm" to show you find the food delicious is not understood by the Chinese. When Larry has made this sound to show his appreciation for his Chinese mother-in-law's culinary prowess, she has responded: "Does that mean he likes it or hates it?" Better to simply say "delicious" or, even better, use the equivalent Chinese expression: "hǎo chī" (how-chir).

Leave a small amount of food on your plate or in your bowl at the end of each course to show you're finished and have had enough. An empty plate or bowl is an invitation for your host to refill it.

Don't ever take the last bit of food on a serving dish, since this will show you are still hungry.

China is generally not a dessert culture, though when they do make something sweet it is usually done with fruit or rice. The last course of a meal is usually fresh fruit. In the summer that usually means watermelon. There are also sweet desserts such as Bā Bǎo Fàn (Eight Treasures Rice) and variations of sweet rice or bean soup.

When you're done eating, place your chopsticks on the table or on the chopstick rest, if one is provided. Never put them across the top of your bowl or, worse yet, stick them straight up in your rice. The former is just bad manners but the latter is strictly taboo because it reminds the Chinese how offerings of vertical incense sticks are traditionally made to the spirits of their dead ancestors . . . definitely bad form for the dinner table.

Drinking

Drinking alcohol at business banquets is common. The greater percentage of Chinese men with whom you make friends will also probably order some alcohol with the meal. There are many brands of Chinese beer and the Chinese always order the large party-size bottles to share. Women

 in China usually do not drink much alcohol. If you're just out with Chinese friends, it's fine for a Western woman to enjoy some beer. But when doing business, women should generally avoid alcohol. If offered some, we suggest that Western businesswomen accept the drink, take a sip, and set it down.

At a banquet or when going out with Chinese friends, the host will offer the first toast. Though the beer may be poured for you, only start drinking *after* the toast. It is not polite to start drinking alone. After the host makes the first toast, anyone can offer a simple toast to people sitting near him or to everyone at the table. Just raising your glass and making eye contact is a sufficient toast.

If you are a woman and do not drink alcohol, use tea or soda or juice for the toast. If you are a man and do not drink alcohol, it is a little harder for the Chinese to accept your toasting with a non-alcoholic beverage, since this might appear to them as insincere. If your principles or the condition of your health really do not permit you to drink any alcohol whatsoever, try to explain why you are drinking tea or juice instead. Not drinking any beverage when a toast is offered would be considered rude.

It is the duty of the host and people seated near the

host—but not the wait staff—to keep refilling everyone else's glasses. If you only want to drink a little beer, be careful to not drain your glass, or else you'll very quickly find that your host or his neighbor has filled it back up for you.

Unlike in American restaurants, tea is not served with the meal unless you request it. It is only served at the end of the meal. If you don't wish a refill, leave your cup rather full to show that you do not want any more.

Conversation

When conversing with your new Chinese friends or business associates, try to keep the following things in mind:

You don't have to keep up a steady patter of conversation all the time. Asians are much more comfortable than Westerners with moments of silence. Remaining silent when you don't have anything important to say shows both politeness and contemplation.

Try to not talk too much about yourself. People from Western countries are all too anxious to tell someone else all about themselves. This seems very self-centered and rude to the Chinese and other Asians. Especially avoid boasting of your accomplishments or bragging about your family members. In Asian society your family members are an extension of yourself. Boasting about them is the same as boasting about oneself. Try to talk instead about matters of common interest.

There are certain things that are considered rude to ask

someone in Western countries but are perfectly acceptable in China. For example, it is not considered impolite to ask someone their age or how much money they make.

It is best to not discuss politics, even if your Chinese friend or business associate brings up the topic. Subjects to avoid include the current leadership, Taiwan, Tibet, and military issues.

Good conversation topics would include the recent modernization of China and its amazing economic growth, the fast pace of change, and the current reforms. Though your knowledge of this may be limited, simply expressing awe and admiration for China today will usually be met with enthusiasm. The Chinese also usually enjoy discussing the differences between China and the West.

Do not be surprised if your Chinese friend or business associate should hesitate when questioned about his or her opinion concerning other issues. China has been a Communist society for many decades now. The Chinese are used to being told what to think by the Communist Party. They have not been encouraged in school or in the workplace to form their own opinions about anything. It is very common to hear a number of people all express an identical opinion independent of one another. For example, these days if you ask the "man on the street" what he thinks of Chairman Mao and the legacy he left behind, do not be surprised if everyone says the same thing: 70% good, 30% bad. After you've asked various Chinese this same question and received exactly the same answer, it finally dawns on you that they're all parroting the government line. Several decades earlier had you asked the same question about Chairman Mao, the general answer would have been: "Just like the First Emperor, Mao ruled with an iron hand but was therefore able to accomplish big things."

Gift Giving

In any culture gift giving helps cement friendships. When making friends in China it is always nice to give your new friend some small present. The gift need not be anything expensive. It's the idea that counts. Preferably you should give something from your home country. Young people would love to receive CDs of popular music or T-shirts, especially ones with English on them. For older people, high-quality pens or picture books of your home state or country make nice gifts. When doing business in China, be aware that officially, gifts are forbidden because of concerns over corruption. Small token gifts, however, are acceptable. It is important that these gifts do not appear to be bribes. Give the top-ranking Chinese associate or client a slightly better gift than the slightly lower-ranking executives with whom you come in contact. Those executives should be given equal gifts of slightly lesser value.

Whether giving presents to a new friend or a business associate, gift items given in multiples of two are representative of good luck and happiness. The number four, however, is unlucky in China, since the word for four and the word for death are homonyms. When giving a present to a new friend, it is not necessary to wrap the present. In a business setting, however, it is best to wrap the present simply or in an attractive box. Do not use white wrapping paper, since white is symbolic of funerals. Taboo gifts include clocks, since the Chinese word for clock, "zhong" (jung), sounds exactly like the word for "the end." Do not give umbrellas, since the word for umbrella is a homonym for the word that means "separation" or "breaking up." Of course, never give as a present any company items, i.e. swag, with the company's logo on it, even if it was expensive and you had to pay for the item yourself. It will appear you are giving your Chinese friend or associate something you received for free.

If you present a card along with a present, be sure not to write on it with red ink. Red ink is often used when writing a "Dear John" or "Dear Mary" letter to end a relationship. Gifts should be given in private to save embarrassment or jealousy.

Offer and receive gifts with both hands. As previously mentioned, it is rude to give or receive almost anything with just one hand, since it literally appears to be "off-handed." It is the custom for the recipient to refuse a gift several times before accepting it, though this is often very subtle and tactfully done. Do not give up just because your friend or associate seems to be reluctant to receive the present. When

invited to someone's home to visit always bring a gift. Appropriate gifts might include any food items or sweets, useful items for the whole family like hand towels or some small gadget, as well as toys or games for any children the family might have. Don't be surprised or disappointed if your friends or associates don't open the present you give them. Gifts are seldom opened in front of the giver. That custom is to save face for the giver should the recipient show any disappointment on opening his or her present.

Dress

China is not a culture where people dress very formally. For daily work life "business casual" is the norm. If you're doing business in China, however, for negotiations as well as scheduled business meetings, formal business attire is expected. For men, a dark-colored, conservative business suit, including a tie, is standard. For women, either a conservative business suit or a dress with a high neckline would be appropriate. Women should avoid displaying too much skin, and should wear flat shoes or shoes with low heels.

There is no restaurant in China where men are expected to wear a coat and tie in order to be allowed in. But the better discos and nightclubs will not allow you to enter if you're wearing a T-shirt, shorts, or tennis shoes. For the disco or club scene you'll need to wear better casual clothes, with slacks for men or women and dress shoes. Always avoid clothes that are too flamboyant or reveal too much skin. Even on the hottest days most Chinese, except younger people in the largest cities, will not wear shorts in public.

Language

It would be best if you could learn a few basic phrases in Chinese before visiting China. If you have no previous knowledge of Chinese, refer to our chapter on speaking Chinese that you will find later in this book. We provide you with basic phrases that you will find very useful. Using them will also help you show that you are making some small effort to speak their language and thereby are showing a measure of respect for the culture you have entered. Since we assume that the majority of our readers do not speak Chinese, when speaking English with Chinese people remember to speak slowly and clearly.

If your Chinese friend or associate does not understand you, it really does not help to speak louder. Just speak more slowly and clearly. Allow some pauses in your speech to make sure the other person is following the gist of what you're saying.

If you're speaking on the phone, be patient with what sounds like silence. If the Chinese person is speaking in English, it is very possible he or she is trying to think of how best to express an idea in your language, which is foreign to them.

Physical Contact and Gestures

Every culture has its own sense of personal space. Americans in particular find the Chinese comfort zone regarding distance a bit too close for their liking. Try to accept that when Chinese converse with you, they might step closer to you than is customary in the West. On the other hand, the Chinese do not like to be touched, especially by strangers. So don't hug, back slap, or put your hand on their arm. You will see people of the same sex walking hand in hand on the street, but that is only for close friends. Finally, never point to someone with your index finger, as Westerners do. Rather use your open hand to gesture in their direction.

12 **Restaurants**

One of the biggest joys in coming to China is to enjoy what is arguably the world's greatest cuisine. Chinese cooking offers a far greater variety of outstanding dishes than any other culture in the world. Realize, though, that "Chinese food" at restaurants in China bears only minimal resemblance to the "Chinese food" you may have encountered in the U.S. For the most part only restaurants in southern China will have Cantonese-style dishes like sweet and sour pork or moo-goo gai-pan. Beijing duck can only really be enjoyed in Beijing. And if, like Larry, you're fond of "ru-shan," fan-shaped fried pieces of goat cheese, then you'll only find it in certain areas of Yunnan Province in the southwest. Every region of China has a large number of its own specialty dishes, most of which are not found on any Chinese-American restaurant menus. And no restaurant in China offers egg rolls or crab Rangoon or even fortune cookies, which are a Western invention.

In China you'll also never find dishes like "Amazing Chicken" or "Shrimp with Assorted Vegetables" or "General Tso's Chicken." Things like "Chop Suey" belong to another

era entirely, a time when Chinese chefs in America were catering to American tastes. After all, Americans generally like
anything that's fried. We also like anything that's sweet. Put
them together, as in "General Tso's Chicken" and you have
a definite winner. Many of the things we order in a Chinese-
American restaurant, such as "Happy Family" or "Three
Delicacies," also reflect the approach to cooking invented by
Chinese-American chefs. That is to say, throw a whole bunch
of vegetables together with one kind of meat or seafood, add
some tasty sauce, and you have a complete meal in one dish.
It's the American preference for one-stop shopping.

Real Chinese food rarely combines more than one type
of meat or seafood with one type of vegetable. Often there is
just one meat or one vegetable stir-fried separately in one of
hundreds of types of sauces. That's because Chinese people
generally order at least five or six different dishes for every
meal in a restaurant. When Americans go out to eat in a restaurant, each person generally orders his or her own single
dish of food. On the other hand, when Chinese people eat
out in a restaurant, many dishes are ordered for the whole
group to enjoy together. Thus, there is no reason to throw every ingredient into one all-purpose dish "chop suey" style.
Because the prices for food in China are so much less than
in countries like the U.S., you can afford to order at least five
or six different dishes for even just two people and still only
end up paying ten U.S. dollars per person.

One of the big mistakes many foreigners make is to limit their dining choices to what can be found in their hotel. While this may be a "safe" choice, most hotel restaurants are generally overpriced and only mediocre in their menu offerings. In anticipation of more tourists, an increasing number of restaurants in most major cities in China are offering English menus, and many new street-savvy guidebooks are moving beyond listing only hotel choices, as was the case when venturing beyond one's hotel was only for the adventurous. The downside is that restaurants can appear quickly and disappear equally quickly in the new, free-enterprise China. It's always helpful to check with your hotel staff to make sure that any restaurants you read about in the guidebooks are still in business. As for asking the hotel staff for a recommendation of a good place to dine, they are often too young and have too thin a wallet to know of the best restaurants in town by personal experience. But sometimes there is a concierge who can recommend the best place to go for dinner outside of the hotel.

A word of advice about reading a menu in a Chinese restaurant. When a dish has an exotic sounding name, you need to find out whether that name is being used poetically or literally. For example, "braised lion heads" are really delicious pork meatballs in a delightful, mildly piquant sauce that you will not want to miss. Similarly "ants climbing the tree" is really a famous if rather simple spicy dish comprised of "cellophane" noodles and bits of ground pork that look a bit like ants.

On the other hand, some dishes have exotic names you must take literally. "Fēngzǐ" or "bee babies" are really roasted bee larvae. They're as yummy as

roasted soybeans, but you should realize that the title of the dish, in this case, is exactly what they are. "Niú biàn," literally, "cow braid," is in fact stewed bull penis. When the restaurant lists "lips of deer " or "monkey brain" you need to take them at their word. "Zhújié chóng," or "bamboo worms" are maggots that look like jointed bamboo. When stir-fried in oil to a golden brown, they're as tasty as French fries. But in order to know what you'll be getting, do ask your waitperson whether you should read the name of the dish literally or figuratively. In the province of Guangdong in the south you really have to be careful. An old adage goes that diners there will eat anything with four legs except a table and anything that flies except an airplane!

There is another curve ball the Chinese will throw a foreign tourist in restaurants. Just because the menu may feature descriptions in English doesn't always mean they will be intelligible. This phenomenon, which can be encountered almost anywhere in China, is a peculiar take-off on English that many simply call "Chinglish," but which we prefer to

call "English Made in China," or "E.M.C." To help you decipher a typical menu in a restaurant in China, we present some excerpts from a menu in the popular tourist town of Lijiang in southwestern China. The restaurant in question is a lovely place situated along a creek in the heart of this eight hundred year old village in the mountains. In the 1990s it was declared a UNESCO World Heritage Site and is now inundated with visitors from all over the world as well as from all over China.

The samples from the menu (below) will give you some idea of how to make sense of and interpret other "E.M.C." menus to be found all over the country.

English version of the Jiannanchun Restaurant menu in Lijiang:

Bin curd → "bean curd", i.e. "tofu"

Ham bowel → "pig intestines"

Fish Soup with Pungent and Tingling Flavor → hot and spicy fish in hot pot

Braided hare → braised hare

Dill picks Fish → dill-pickled fish

Fried chicken and Chinese Chest Nuts

Bouilli → i.e., "red-cooked pork"

Fried Rabbit Meat with Wild Prickle → fried rabbit with wild mountain peppers

Wild Prickle Made Chicken Paws → wild mountain peppers with chicken feet

Couple Lung Pieces → i.e., "Husband and wife pork lung slices"

Rabbit Cubes with Chilly Oil → "cooked in oil flavored with hot chili peppers"

Tasty Cooked Peanut → i.e., fried peanuts

A Class Yun cigaret → a class "A" cigarette from Yunnan Province

Melon Pork Chip Soup → i.e., soup with winter melon and pork slices

Purely Stewed Beef Soup → soup with stewed beef ribs

Deep Fried Bee Cocoons

Stewed Chicken with Chinese Caterpillar Fungus

Deep Fried Dragonflies

While there's nothing particularly funny about the last three dishes, these are examples of dishes you must take literally.

English Made in China

In the previous chapter we introduced the concept of "E.M.C.," or "English Made in China." With over 100 million foreign tourists coming to China each year, China is considerately putting up more and more signs in English as well as Chinese. This all seems very reassuring until you soon realize that the English they're using is not the English you've been taught. It's not the King's or Queen's English, either. In fact, it's quite unlike any English known to man or woman. Playing on the famous slogan, you could refer to it as "English with Chinese Characteristics."

The sample restaurant menu in the previous chapter is just one example of encountering "E.M.C." There are signs in airports, in parks, in museums, on packages of snack food, all of which employ this Chinese version of English. Here are some examples:

Airports

Sign in Beijing Airport:

No entry in peacetime (i.e., Emergency Exit only)

Kunming Airport Security sign:

> *No controlled dirks;*
> *No in Flam Mables*
> *No Truncheons*

Sign in Xian Airport over a store that is the only authorized seller of certain goods:

> *Monopoly Shop*

Trains

Sign on train washroom between Beijing and Tianjin:

> *No occupying while stabling* (i.e., don't use when train is in the station)

Cablecars

Sign by the cablecar in Kunming for the International Horticultural Gardens:

> *Armymen teachers and retiring people rely on credentials concerned can have 5 yuan preferential treatment. The oldmen over 70 yrs. old peaple of heart diease, hypertension deformity and fearing high politely refuse to take cable car.* (faithfully reprinted complete with original typos)

Taxicabs

Notice in back seat of taxi in Kunming, with picture of a fox, asking if you know which animal it is:

> *The policemen remind you:*

Please remember the animal's name and code. Please don't leave
anything in the car.

Hotels

Guest information booklet for the Bell Tower Hotel in Xian:

"The recreation and fitness department lies in the 2nd floor, offer
sauna massage in 24 hrs. to you, cosmetology, idle amusement ser-
vice, that chess and card, etc. are repaired, luxurious environment,
hospitable service, awaits your presence.

The great kindness and support of the recreation and fitness
dept. specially pursue the favorable activity for guests in order to
thank for guests long-term, the service is not reduced, it is more to
be favorable. Welcome your presence again."

Sign for massage in four-star hotel:

Massage:
Pull out the fire bottle
Medicine the wash foot
Degeneration of the parts of the vertebrae

Card in a room in the Bell Tower Hotel, Xian, warning
against outside "massage" services:

In order to ensure your safety of human life and property,
if receive the message (meaning "massage") *service*
telephone that the hotel external world offers, please
refuse.

Restaurants

Sign in Xian teahouse:

> *melon seeds, peanuts, nosh 3 yuan plate* (note: "nosh" is the Yiddish word for "snack")

Paper cover for disposable chopsticks:

> *For your health Please use sanitanen chopsticks* (i.e., sanitized chopsticks)

Packaged Food Items

In a gift shop in the Xian airport on a box of chocolates in the shape of the terra-cotta warriors in the First Emperor's tomb:

> *Qin Terra-Cotta is one biggest buring mount of the Qin Shi Huang Mausoleum. It is composed by Chariots, Cavalryman, Infantry-man, Including the General officer.*
>
> *All these Terra-Cotta have different facial expression, various dressing.*
>
> *They were arranged in the military formation which provides the best material for the study of Qin Dynasty's army. Our chocolate is the copy of the Terra-Cotta army.*

On a package of cookies given on domestic flights in China:

> *Increase into the real object material of original flavor, through dispensing of*
>> *Science, in really ideal good product that enjoy of*
> *delicacy.*

Parks and Gardens

Sign at entrance to Heilongtan Park in Lijiang, Yunnan Province:

> *Which to below 1.3 m child, holding the disabled card, holding the retired card personnel and 70 yr. old of above old person should give free of them, to the serviceman, the student which has the corresponding credential should give the half-price preferential treatment.*

Sign in the Hanshan Temple of Suzhou:

> *Conscientiously maintain public hygiene.*
> *No spitting, pissing, shitting, or littering at wrong places.*
> *No fight, gambling, or hooliganism.*

Sign in national park of Jiuzhaigou:

> *Retiring area* (i.e., rest area for tourists)

Tourist brochure for Jiuzhaigou National Park:

> *Next to Jiuzhaigou Valley and Huanglong, the counties of Mao-xian and Wenchuan are the place where the Zang and Qiang nationality live together. The wood-board houses and barbicans are distributed in the green mountain and waters. The local people are*

homeliness and soul-
ful and hospitality
to guests. If you are
agreed, you may
be a guest of their
family. You must
get candies ready
for the children, and you
may be welcome. Buttered tea is one of the main foods. June 6 of the
lunar calendar every year is the Temple Fair Day of Huanglong
Temple, when thousands of people from all directions gather here,
having a jolly time.

Museums and Historic Sites

Sign on Xian History Museum:
*Temporary exhibitions which offer freshness to the
viewers.*

Captions by art work in the Xian History Museum:
A making up concubine (Ming painting of a courtesan apply-
ing makeup)
Pottery figure of an unfree peasant (figurine of a farmer)

Theaters

Pamphlet for audience in theatre in Xian:
This show translates the marrow of the traditional culture with

modern arctic ideal and showing method. The theatre with the ultra open consciousness, the modern bearing and the compatability with the world which became meny-faceted, face to the head of state, official business, tour and social contact, technical communication, leisure and entertainment etc. all kinds of consumers.

Pearl of the Orient Tower in Shanghai

The ragamuffin, drunken people and psychotics are forbidden to enter the Tower.

No smoking at non-appointed spot.

Prohibit carrying tinder and explosive (banger, match, lighter), restricted cutter (kitchen knife, scissors, fruit knife, sword, and so on), and metal-made electric appliance.

Prohibit carrying the animals and articles which disturb the common sanitation (including the peculiar smell of effluvium).

Prohibit carrying the articles which can destroy and pollute inner environment of the Tower.

Prohibit carrying dangerous germs, pests, and other baleful biology. Forbid any articles from epidemic areas.

Prohibit hanging streamer, slogan, and any other prints in the Tower, including commerce, politics, religion and so on.

The cubage of liquid article which the tourist carries can't overage one milliliter and must accept examination. . . .

Learning Chinese

Despite China's rich history and civilization, the Chinese language is not that difficult to learn. For one thing, there are no difficult rules of conjugation to master as in Western languages. Instead of saying "I see, you see, he/she sees" the Chinese say "Wǒ kàn, nǐ kàn, tā kàn." The word "Tā" (he or she) denotes both masculine and feminine in spoken Chinese.

Because there is no conjugation, there is no use of tense in Chinese either. Instead of saying, "I saw her yesterday" the Chinese simply say, "I yesterday see she." Since we're talking about yesterday, it is what we call "past tense." There is no declension. Instead of saying, "I see her; she sees me" the Chinese simply say the equivalent of "I see she; she see I."

Chinese is a tonal language. That means that you must make your voice go up or down to change the meaning of a word. Mandarin Chinese, the dialect that has been the "national language" for many centuries, fortunately only has four different tones. Each word you learn will use one of those tones. Count your blessings. Had Cantonese been chosen as the national language, you would have had to learn six tones. Four tones are enough to handle, thank you very much.

Fortunately we have the same four tones or intonations in English. The difference is that how we intone a word in English doesn't completely change the definition of the word, only the feeling behind it. Consider the sound "oh" for example. If we say the word "oh" with a high, level pitch, sustaining it for a second or two, as in "ooohhh, that's great!" we have the "first tone" in Chinese. This can be indicated by a tone mark, which is a line running over the vowel of the word to indicate its tone, or by a number in parentheses immediately following the word:

> First tone: ¯ flat tone
> Second tone: ´ rising tone
> Third tone: ˇ downward before rising up
> Fourth tone: ` sharp downward tone

If we say the same sound "oh" with a rising intonation, as if we're asking the question "oh, is that so?" then we have the second tone in Mandarin Chinese. If we offer sympathy to someone by saying "oh" with a falling intonation but with our voice rising back up at the end, as in "oh, that's too bad," we have the third tone in Chinese. Finally if we say "oh" with our voice starting fairly high up and falling, as in "oh, that's cool," we have the fourth and final tone of Chinese. Make sure that when you learn a word in Chinese you learn the correct tone, or you could be in big trouble. Unlike in English, when you change the tone of a word in Chinese, it completely changes

the dictionary definition of a word as well as the "character" or "pictograph" with which it's written.

Here are some examples of the difference a tone can make to a word.

Let's take the famous example of the sound "ma." Now in almost every language of the world "ma" means "mother." It does in Chinese, too, but only if you pronounce "ma" with the first tone. If you say "ma" with the second or "rising" tone, it means "marijuana!" If you say it with the third tone, "ma" means "horse." Now, you don't want to go calling your mother a horse, do you?! If you say "ma" with the fourth or "falling" tone, then you've changed the meaning once again, this time to "curse; scold; yell at."

Here is a full Chinese sentence. See if you can figure out what it means. We'll indicate which tone you need to use. For example: "mā mà mǎ." So what does that mean? Of course, any Chinese person can tell you that "Mom yelled at the horse." Now, we don't know exactly what the horse did to make Mom so mad, but it must have been something

pretty bad. We suggest you don't try the same shenanigans as that horse!

Here's another example of the importance of saying the tones correctly. A young American is studying elementary Chinese with a lovely young Chinese woman. He says: "Wo yao wen ni," (I want to ask you), but he's not sure of the tone for the word "wen," which means "to ask." So he tries the second tone and says: Wó yaò wén nǐ. Unfortunately "wen" with the second tone means "to smell." Oops. The young woman shakes her head. The young man realizes that he's said the tone wrong and tries another tone instead. This time he says emphatically: Wó yaò wěn nǐ (I want to kiss you). "Wen" with the third tone means to kiss. The young woman is about to leave the room. Finally in desperation the young man shouts out: Wó yaò wèn nǐ. Ah, the fourth tone did it. "What do you want to ask me?" the young woman finally replies, much relieved.

We offer below a short list of the top 20 phrases we suggest you learn for your time in China. Learning these won't make you able to discuss in Chinese the re-valuation of the Chinese yuan vis-à-vis the American dollar. But they will help you get your basic needs met. Pay particular attention to the tones of the words! By trying to speak at least a few words in Chinese, you're showing some respect for the Chinese culture by caring enough to have learned at least a little of the language.

There are also no plurals in Chinese. Instead of saying "one mouse; two mice" or "one house; two houses" the Chinese just say the equivalent of "one mouse; two mouse" or "one house; two house." Blessedly there is no noun gender in Chinese, written or spoken. This is a relief after studying languages such as Spanish or French, where you have to figure out whether a table, for instance, is masculine or feminine, depending presumably on how shapely the legs are.

If Chinese is so simple, then why don't all Americans pick it up as fast as they learn to use a cell phone? One factor is the fact that there are almost no cognates between Chinese and English. That is to say that there are very few words in Chinese that sound like their equivalent in English. Around 60% of words in French or Spanish have words that sound somewhat similar to the word with the same meaning in English. That's because of our common Latin roots.

In Chinese, a hamburger is a "hànbǎobāo" ("hahn-bow-bow, with the "bow" pronounced as in "to bow before a king"). Coca-Cola is "kěkǒukělè" ("kuh-koh-kuh-luh" = "pleases mouth, can have joy"). And a computer is, of course, "diàn-nǎo" ("dien-now"), literally "electric brain." In other words, if you want to learn some Chinese, you'll have to forget about getting any help from English or French or German. You'll need to learn to make some strange sounds that will be totally unfamiliar to you.

One of the particular joys of speaking Chinese with Chinese people is their delight that a foreigner can say anything at all in their language beyond "nǐ haǒ" ("knee how"), meaning "hello." As a foreign tourist in Paris or Berlin you have to speak French or German very well indeed to impress the natives, but in China you get big strokes as a foreigner just for being able to say just a few phrases in Chinese. Chinese is so different from Western languages that few Western tourists ever bother to learn even one word of it.

Here are our top Chinese phrases: (We first give the standard transliteration in pinyin, followed by our own transliteration in parentheses to help you with the pronunciation). Note that there are some instances when the same character is repeated twice, the tone of the second character is dropped.

Hello → *nǐ haǒ* → Pronounced as "knee how."
  (Think: How's your knee, i.e. "How are you?")

Thank you → *xiè xie* → Pronounced as "syeh syeh"
  (The second "xie" has no tone.)

You're welcome → *bú kè qi* → boo kuh chee
  (The "chee" has no tone.)

Good morning → *zaǒ shàng haǒ* → dzow shahng how

Please stand in line → *qǐng páiduì* → ching pie dway

Too expensive → *tài guì le* → tie gway luh

(Make it) cheaper → *piányi yìdiǎn* → pien yee ee dien

(I; we) don t want it → *búyào* → boo yow

I want this one → *wǒ yào zheìge* → waw yow jay guh
    (note: "guh" has no tone!)

How much (does it cost)? → *duóshaǒ* → dwo shao

Where is the bathroom? → *cèsuǒ zaì nǎlǐ* → tsuh swo
dz-eye nah lee

Over there → *nàli* → nah lee
    (note: "lee" has no tone)

Please give me → *qǐng geǐ wǒ* → ching gay waw

Fine; O.K.; good; alright → *haǒ* → how

Not O.K.; no good → *bùhaǒ* → boo how

I want to go (show taxi driver the address in Chinese)
→ *Wǒ yào qù* → waw yow chee-you

**(Want) to go to _____ (e.g. when buying tickets at train
or bus station)** → *Wǒ yào daò _____ qù* → waw you
dow _____ chee-you

Police! (in case of theft or emergency) → *jǐngchá!* →
jing chah!

Faster! → *kuaì yìdiǎn!* → kweye ee dien!

Numbers one through ten:

one → *yī* → ee

two → *èr* → ar

three → *sān* → sahn

four → *sì* → szih

five → *wǔ* → woo

six → *liù* → leo

seven → *qī* → chee

eight → *bā* → bah

nine → *jiǔ* → geo

ten → *shí* → sure

One of something → *eē guh*

Two of something → *lee-ǎng guh*

Three of something → *sāhn guh*

Etc.

One of the first things you'll notice when you arrive in China is that everywhere you look there are signs in some kind of hieroglyphic writing that looks very much like chicken tracks. Your first hunch is that some practical joker has replaced all the English or some other reasonable alphabetic language with some made-up pictures. Then you remember reading that the Chinese have their own "inscrutable" written language that is said to date back some four or five thousand years.

Of course, most Americans have seen Chinese "characters" in the U.S. We see them on storefronts in our Chinatowns as well as on some Chinese restaurant menus. We see them on T-shirts, because we consider Chinese characters beautiful and fascinating and maybe a bit mysterious. There are even Chinese characters tattooed on the bodies of our NBA basketball stars. Allen Iverson, the star of the Philadelphia 76ers, has the Chinese pictograph "zhōng" (juhng), or "loyalty," tattooed on his neck. Marcus Camby of the New York Knicks has two Chinese characters tattooed on one of his arms. The characters literally mean "compelled tribe," which isn't correct Chinese. But who cares? Chinese characters are cool to most of us for the very fact that we don't understand them. It's the mystery that attracts us. And they are much prettier than any alphabet.

Actually the Chinese writing system is one of the great wonders of the world. Originally, all writing, such as hieroglyphics and cuneiform, was based on pictographs. Chinese, however, is the only non-alphabetical language that has stood the test of time and is still used today. The Japanese borrowed the Chinese writing system in the sixth century and also continue to use it.

The problem for foreign tourists, however, is that most of them don't read Chinese. They don't know whether the sign is telling them to turn right or left to go to the restroom. They don't even know if the characters they think mean "restroom" might be the characters for "pool hall" or "tanning booth."

Here are some of the most common signs you want to recognize when out and about anywhere in China.

厕所 → *cèsuǒ* → Pronounced as "tsuh-swoh" → **toilet**
  (literally "convenience place")

男 → *nán* → **men's room**

女 → *nǚ* → **ladies' room**

入口 → *rù kǒu* → **entrance**
  (literally "entering mouth")

出口 → *chū kǒu* → **exit**
  (literally "leaving mouth")

售票处 → *shòupiàochù* → **ticket window**
  (literally "selling tickets place")

出租车 → *chūzūchē* → **taxicab**
  (literally "out rent car")

Going Home

This book began by showing you what you may encounter when arriving at an airport in China. The only things you really need to worry about are getting through immigration and navigating the airport restrooms. Getting out of China, even at the same airport at which you arrived, can be a totally different experience.

On international flights out of China, you are allowed two suitcases for check in weighing up to 32 kilos (70 lbs) total. Your luggage will be weighed and if you exceed the weight limit, you will be required to pay a fine. Usually this is done at a separate ticket counter within the departure terminal, and you will need to bring the receipt of payment back to the airline representative before your luggage can be processed or put on the conveyor. Be aware, however, that on domestic flights within China, the baggage restrictions are much more severe. If you are flying economy class, you may be charged a hefty fee for any luggage exceeding 20 kilos (44 lbs); if you are flying business class, the limit is 30 kilos (66 lbs), and, in a blow to egalitarianism, first class travelers are allowed a whopping 40 kilos (88 lbs) per person. If you're

even five pounds over the allowed weight, you could end up paying as high a penalty as the whole ticket cost. Usually this is not the case, and fortunately, if you are traveling as a couple or a family, the airlines will average the weight of all your checked luggage. If the average weight of each passenger's bag is only 20 kilograms, you're fine. One trick is to put all your heaviest items in your backpack or some other carry-on item. You should be aware, however, that you're only allowed one carry-on item, not counting your camera or purse. And the carry-on can't exceed five kilos (a little over 10 lbs).

China's new airports are remarkably efficient, but in a land of 1.3 billion, let's face it: there can be screw-ups. On a recent domestic flight within China, we got up at 5:00 A.M. in order to take a cab from our mountain village in Sichuan Province. For two hours we bounded along a winding road in the midst of mile-high mountains close to the Tibet border. Tired and carsick, we were relieved to reach the airport early, arriving at 8:00 A.M. to catch our 9:30 A.M. flight to the provincial capital of Chengdu.

We were holding tickets but needed to get boarding passes and it took us an excruciatingly long time to reach the ticket counter because several large tour groups had arrived just a moment before, jamming up all the available ticket agents. After waiting for at least thirty minutes, our turn finally came. We handed our tickets to the airline representative. We were then told that our Chinese travel agency, the largest in China, had apparently failed to confirm *one* of our tickets. It was Larry's. So we had one good ticket for the flight out. Since airlines routinely oversell their flights, this meant that all the available seats were taken by members of the large tour group in front of us. We panicked, but the airline representative shoved one ticket back to us with all the concern she would have shown had we told her the Chicago White Sox had failed to win the 1959 World Series.

When we insisted she do something for us, she finally agreed to put us on the next flight out. She handed us our boarding passes and, relieved, we started to go through security. We immediately turned back, however, when we realized that our bags had been checked through on the flight from which we had been dropped. We wanted our luggage to be on the same plane with us, since we had to pick them up for a connecting flight. So Qin had to go back behind the counter into the baggage security area to find our suitcases, bring them back out, and have them properly re-tagged for the new flight. Of course, this meant having the bags x-rayed again. This time, the security workers spotted something odd in Qin's bag. It turned out to be a can of hair spray.

We headed once again to the gate entrance, ready to sail through security. They wouldn't let Larry through, however. That was because the boarding pass the woman had given Larry didn't have his name, Lawrence Roy Herzberg, on it. No, the name on the boarding pass was Samuel Luk Wong. We already knew that Chinese travel agencies or airlines often misspell foreigners' names. In fact, there is a rule that says if fewer than three letters of your name are misspelled on your airline ticket and/or boarding pass, it's O.K. It doesn't have to completely match the name on your passport. Qin had gone through China taking domestic flights where her name on her ticket always read Qing Herzber instead of Qin Herzberg. No problem. Only two letters in the name on her ticket differed from her passport. But Samuel Luk Wong was more than three letters different from Lawrence Roy Herzberg!

Larry had to go back and stand in line again so that he could get a boarding pass that actually had his name on it. No apology or explanation was given. When he was given his boarding pass, Larry had naively assumed that it would have his name on it. Always check your boarding pass to make sure all the information is correct.

There's another potential snafu of which you should be aware, one that on our last trip to China almost made us miss our flight back to the U.S. There are two Shanghai airports. Now that in and of itself should not be particularly surprising. After all, the Shanghai metropolitan area, with at least 17 million people, is China's largest city. America's largest city, New York, has two airports, namely Kennedy and La Guardia. There are two airports in both Paris and London. It only makes sense that Shanghai, which along with Beijing is the biggest hub for both international and domestic travel in China, should also have two airports. The only problem is that travel agents in the West are not always aware of which airport it is when they are making a booking; if they see "Shanghai" that's good enough for them, but it may put you in a bit of a pinch.

What we didn't notice until the previous day was that our flight from Xiamen to Shanghai was scheduled to arrive at the Shanghai Hongqiao Airport, where most domestic flights land, but that our flight back to the U.S. would leave from the newer Shanghai Pudong Airport, which handles all international flights. The airports are separated by exactly 50 kilometers (about 30 miles). For us, that meant negotiating 30 miles of congested highway and clogged roads in China's biggest city. Our travel agent back home in the States had only allowed two hours from our arrival time until our international flight home was scheduled to depart, not realizing two different Shanghai airports were involved.

Fortunately we were able to contact the local Chinese travel agent in Xiamen, who booked us on a much earlier flight to Shanghai, so we could make the connection easily. We got on the 1½ hour flight from Xiamen to Shanghai Hongqiao and arrived five hours before our flight took off from Shanghai Pudong airport to the U.S. Everything seemed OK, but we should have known better. The Murphy of "Murphy's Law" would have loved it in China. Anything really can and really will go wrong. As is true with so many domestic flights within China, the plane will not always taxi to the gate. Instead it leaves you out on the tarmac, where you exit down a moveable stairway to a waiting shuttle bus to take you to the terminal. We crowded on to the shuttle, the doors closed, and we were waiting to make the two minute ride to the gate when a big commotion suddenly arose.

A middle-aged man started yelling that he couldn't find the big bundle of money he had put in his bag in the overhead compartment of the plane. Someone on the plane had definitely stolen his money during the flight, he claimed. When he went to exit the aircraft, he discovered that his bag in the overhead compartment was partially open and the gloves which had been inside had fallen to the floor of the plane. Airline employees ran frantically back into the plane to search and in the meantime a police car drove up. Our shuttle bus was going nowhere as an investigation ensued.

A policeman got on the shuttle bus and started questioning the man and the people around him. As the minutes went by, one Chinese man started shouting that he would gladly waive his right against being searched so that he could be cleared and go on his way without further delay, and tried to convince others to do the same. Time dragged on, with the Chinese passengers on the shuttle growing more and more impatient. The four other foreigners on the bus besides Qin and Larry did not understand at all the drama that was being played out, and just stared uncomprehendingly at the shouting Chinese passengers.

When it was hinted that all the passengers might be searched and their carry-on items examined, the man who had lost his money started shouting that he had found his money on the floor of the shuttle bus. Obviously the police ruse had worked and the thief in his panic had dropped the envelope with the money which he had pilfered. In today's China, Communist state that it is, citizens cannot be searched arbitrarily by police—at least not so publicly as this would have been.

In any case we were free to go. Once again, however, we were reminded that travel in China can always throw unexpected obstacles in your path, even when everything seems to be going swimmingly.

If your flight in China is cancelled or seems to be delayed indefinitely, do not panic or try to exchange your tickets for another flight. Frankly, it's just too much of a hassle to retrieve your bags, stand in line to change your tickets, try to find a hotel near the airport for the night, and then contact the people who were supposed to pick you up and won't know that you didn't stick with your original flight.

Assuming your bags are now checked through and now you only need to pass through Security and Immigration before heading to your gate. You see there is a form you need to fill out for leaving China. It's a simple form. All you have to do is write your name, passport number, flight number, purpose of your stay in China. What the form doesn't tell you, and no person or guidebook does either, is that you must use BLUE or BLACK ink. For 99% of the flying public, that may not be a problem. But many of us Americans these days like to use pens with red ink, or purple ink, or green ink, or even yellow ink. Larry happened to have a pen with red ink. He's a professor, after all. Many of us in the teaching trade get a thrill from marking up our students' papers and tests with red ink. So Larry, on his umpteenth time flying out of China, filled out his form in red ink in beautiful block letters.

When he reached the Immigration counter and proudly presented his U.S. passport along with his beautifully hand-printed form, the officer said in gruff, barely understandable English: "No good. Led ink. Led ink." When Larry clarified in Chinese that his form was unacceptable because it was printed in red ink, Larry asked where it was written on the form or anywhere else that red ink was no good. Just policy, he was told. After 25 years of teaching college Chinese Larry still didn't know what every Chinese knows. Red ink is only used in China to correct mistakes. So teachers use it to grade students' homework, just like we do. It's never used for business transactions, or, appar-

ently, for something so simple and seemingly innocuous as an Immigration form.

Caught off-guard and in a bit of a huff, Larry asked where he could get a blue or black pen. The Immigration official pointed to a pen affixed to a nearby table. The trouble was that there was an old Chinese man filling out forms for himself and his wife, and he was filling them out with the greatest care. When Larry finally spotted another pen he could use, he traced over the red ink with the blue ink of the pen provided. He then returned to the Customs counter. "No good," the man said in Chinese this time. "Led ink!" "But I traced over it . . . " "No good," Larry was told. Larry got a new form and filled it out all over again in blue ink. The information wasn't any different than the first time. But the color was right.

Larry finally caught up to his wife 15 minutes later at the gate. After preaching to students for 25 years about how wonderful China was, and how they should all think of going there someday to study or to work, Larry suddenly was there at the gate shouting to his wife: "I hate this country! I'm never coming back!!" One month later, of course, he's already planning his next trip to China with some of his students. He had remembered all the reasons that had attracted him to China in the first place.

So Why Go to China?

If there are so many minor hassles to overcome in traveling to and around China, why bother to go there? Because, in spite of every small inconvenience or aggravation we've experienced in our many trips to China, for every minute we spent in anger or frustration, there were many hours or even days when we were enjoying an exciting or lovely time and didn't want to be anywhere else. That's because there is so much of value to experience in the Middle Kingdom. There is the long and richly patterned history that is preserved in its multitude of historic sites. There are the many breathtaking mountain ranges and rivers that make China one of the most scenically spectacular places on the planet. And there is without question the world's most varied and delicious cuisine.

But it is more than that, a lot more. There are the sights, smells, and sounds of a dynamic society with an energy and buzz of activity that has accompanied the new economic freedoms and prosperity. There is a sense of limitless possibilities in an era that has seen the fastest economic growth of any society in history. Then there are the people, possibly

the most warm, welcoming, and good-humored of all the peoples in Asia. So many of them are amazingly brilliant, talented, and just plain wonderful. Since China has over one-fifth of the world's people, it is only natural that the country should also have over one-fifth of the world's best and most gifted people. Finally there is the fact that, given the tremendous size of both its land and its population, coupled with its rapid economic growth, China is the emerging superpower that some day may soon rival the United States. We foreigners have a feeling that if a country is that important in the world, we need to understand it better than most of us currently do.

We hope you'll visit China sometime soon. We think you'll have an extraordinary experience. Just be prepared for the many little pitfalls we've mentioned in this book and try to follow our advice, and you'll have a great time. And remember that whether you travel to China or anywhere else in the world, along with your deodorant always bring a healthy sense of humor.

Happy traveling!

Topic Index

ABOUT THE AUTHORS

Larry Herzberg is a professor at Calvin College in Grand Rapids, Michigan. Since 1984, he has taught first- through fourth-year Chinese language courses, as well as several courses on Chinese culture and society. He has visited mainland China numerous times over the past 25 years, most recently with 12 of his students on a study tour during the summer of 2007. Larry is also a full-time violinist with the Grand Rapids Symphony.

Qin Xue Herzberg grew up in Beijing and is a graduate of Beijing Normal University, where she majored in Chinese literature. For the past ten years she has taught upper-level Chinese language courses at Calvin College. She has written articles for several of China's most popular magazines, including *Marriage and the Family* and *China Educator's Journal*. She has also published articles in America's leading Chinese newspaper, *World Journal*.

Larry and Qin have produced a 60-minute documentary for schools and educators entitled "China Today: Issues That Trouble Americans at the Start of the 21st Century," which was released in 2008 and is available from the Calvin Media Foundation of Calvin College.

The couple have received a grant to return to China in the summer of 2009 to film a documentary with interviews concerning how the Chinese people view their country as well as the U.S., juxtaposed with interviews with Americans on how they view China